*Etty Hillesum*

# Etty Hillesum
## A life transformed

*Patrick Woodhouse*

continuum

**Published by Continuum**
The Tower Building, 11 York Road, London SE1 7NX
80 Maiden Lane, Suite 704, New York NY 10038

www.continuumbooks.com

First published 2009

British Library Cataloguing-in-Publication Data
A catalogue record for this book is available from the British Library.

ISBN 97818470642643

Typeset by Kenneth Burnley, Wirral, Cheshire
Printed and bound by MPG Books, Cornwall

# Contents

Etty in her room, c. 1937–8

*Collection Jewish Historical Museum, Amsterdam*

'I knew that I would have to undergo many transformations.'

*(Etty Hillesum, 27th July 1942)*

The Watchtower at Westerbork today

*Patrick Woodhouse*

# Foreword

*By the Archbishop of Canterbury*

The publication (initially in 1986) of the journals and letters of Etty Hillesum made available an utterly distinctive modern chronicle of conversion: a *Confessions of St Augustine* for our own day. Because it is for our own day, however, it is not simply a story of someone finding their way to a settled traditional allegiance. And because of its setting, in the midst of the atrocities of the Holocaust – because this is the history of a young woman killed in Auschwitz at the age of 29 – we could hardly expect it to be anything like a consoling record of homecomings and solutions. Not, of course, that Augustine's great work is that kind of record at all – and Etty Hillesum's texts can perhaps help us read that and similar classics with a new eye for their complexities and unfinished business. But here is a quintessentially modern mind and sensibility gradually being changed in such a way that there is no escape, not only from speaking *about* God, but no escape from the challenge to speak *for* God.

Those who have read the published letters and diaries will know what an exceptional witness they give to the dawning of God in someone's awareness, but thus far there have been relatively few discussions of the recurring themes. We need help in tracing the patterns, and help too in connecting this passionate and idiosyncratic voice with the more familiar idioms of traditional faith and practice – without in the process so domesticating her that she ceases to give the unequivocally contemporary witness that makes her so extraordinary.

In this book, Patrick Woodhouse has offered just such help, respectful at every point of Etty's distinctiveness and not trying to make her an 'orthodox' martyr. Anyone studying her with the help of these pages will emerge convinced that she can properly stand with Simone Weil and Dietrich Bonhoeffer and Maria Skobtsova as a signal representative of what has been called the 'death-cell philosophy' of the twentieth century: the discovery of a real and completely, powerfully transforming divine faithfulness, present even in the depths of the nightmare of totalitarian inhumanity. Etty Hillesum deserves to be read far more deeply and extensively than she has been thus far, and this book is a clear and moving invitation to such a deeper and more sustained reading.

+ *Rowan Cantuar:*
Lambeth Palace
S Teresa of Avila, 2008

# Introduction

On 9th March 1941, a 27-year-old Dutch Jew named Etty Hillesum – living in enemy-occupied Amsterdam – made her first entry in a diary, which, together with the letters she later wrote from a transit camp, became one of the most remarkable set of documents to emerge from the Nazi Holocaust. They tell the story of a life, which, in just two and a half years, was entirely transformed.

The dark and ever-threatening background to the diary are the terrible events of the Nazi persecution of the Jews, which at that time was sweeping across Europe. In July 1942 this persecution was to take this young woman into Westerbork, the transit camp for Dutch Jews on their way to the east; and eventually, in September 1943, to Auschwitz, where she died.

Under the pressure of these appalling events and through a relationship with an unusual Jungian therapist who had a huge influence upon her, Etty was to emerge as an inspirational figure: inspirational for those who knew her at the time and with whom she shared the suffering of the transit camp, and inspirational for all whose lives, through her diary and letters, she has touched since. Through her vivid writing we meet a young woman who shaped and lived a spirituality of hope in the darkest period of the twentieth century.

Following the narrative of her life, the book begins by exploring the process of personal change that occurred in her as she emerged from an insecure and chaotic past. As her confidence grew and she discovered a more integrated self, she began to talk about a sense of

'God' and to pray. She describes herself as 'the girl who could not kneel' and yet 'who learned to pray'. It was, at first, hesitant and faltering, and she was embarrassed by it, but slowly her growing inner life to which she constantly returned became all important to her, sustaining her more and more as the persecution intensified and the world around her darkened. As the noose tightened, and the realization grew in her that her people were helpless and faced an inevitable destruction, a new and intimate understanding of God was born in her heart.

It was her rich spiritual imagination and the sense of inner depth which colours all her writing, which enabled her, amidst the evil and suffering that she describes so graphically, to see the world differently. In the hellish conditions of the camp she continued to insist, extraordinarily, that life is meaningful and good. How could this be? She was not mad. Under the pressure of the suffering she did not become detached from reality – for she describes everything around her so vividly: the overcrowding, the mud, the cruelty, the traumatized broken people, the weekly cattle-truck train taking its pitiful load of exhausted humanity away to 'the east', from where they were never heard from again – she is the chronicler of it all. But despite everything, she continued to have a deep sense of the goodness and beauty of life.

Above all else that was remarkable about her, Etty Hillesum refused to hate. While others around her dealt with their fear and reinforced their resistance by hatred of the German occupiers, Etty refused to hate, and she held to this conviction to the end.

Her courageous story leads into profound understandings about the nature of God and how suffering and sorrow can be redemptive, not destructive. These emerged out of the struggles of her inner life, and the insights she arrived at were not easily gained. What we witness in the diary, and through her letters to her friends, is a battle to go on living with hope and integrity even as the world around her collapses. Her greatest weapons in this are her love of people, her deep sense of God within, and her passion for truth.

As death approached, the faith that she held to so courageously became everything to her. But, perhaps surprisingly, Etty was not a 'religious' person – at least not in the institutional sense of that word. She belonged to neither synagogue nor church and shows no interest whatever in institutional religion. Her route to God was initially through psychotherapy and an exhaustive, relentless and disciplined grappling with the self, which led to the discovery of the hidden inner depths of the human soul.

This makes her a woman for our time, when institutional religion is in decline and yet the hunger for authentic spirituality is more keenly felt than ever. Etty speaks across the boundaries of religions, pointing to a way of being human that transcends such divisions and overcomes the evils of violence and hatred. It was a way that was tested to the uttermost and shone through under the most terrible circumstances imaginable. Her story rekindles confidence that the way of faith is not, as so many sceptical voices in today's world suggest, an absurd and misguided delusion.

Remarkably, however, nearly 70 years after her death, this story still remains comparatively unknown. The explanation for this lies with the diaries and letters themselves. For almost 40 years after her death they remained unpublished. Before she finally left for the transit camp, Etty had handed her Amsterdam diaries over to a friend, Maria Tuinzing, asking that, if she should not return, they be passed to the writer Klaas Smelik with the request that they be published.

After the war, Klaas Smelik attempted to find a publisher but without success. In late 1979 his son, Klaas A. D. Smelik, who had inherited the diaries and letters from his father, asked the publisher J. G. Gaarlandt to look at them. This resulted in an edited version of the diaries being published in Dutch in October 1981 (the English version came out in 1983). This book – *An Interrupted Life* – made Etty's name known. Gaarlandt published two further selections of her writings in 1982 and 1984, but still approximately half of the diary and some letters remained unpublished.

It was not until 1986 that the full texts of all the diaries and all the then known letters came out when the complete and unabridged letters and diaries were published in Dutch. The English version of this book: *Etty: The Letters and Diaries of Etty Hillesum 1941–1943, Complete and Unabridged*, was published in 2002.

Together with notes at the back which provide a comprehensive literary, biographical and historical commentary on the text, plus an index, this substantial scholarly work is the basis for understanding her life and writings. However, it is large and detailed, it runs to 800 pages, and so is not easily accessible to the modern reader.

Drawing on that work, the present book aims to present in an accessible way the story of the two and half years of her life which the diary and letters reveal, and to reflect on the meaning of that story.

The book explores her chaotic childhood, her relationship with her therapist Julius Spier and her discovery of her self. It looks at how her journey of faith began and how it developed. It explores the reasons behind her steadfast refusal to hate and the consequences of that moral stance. It examines her choice not to hide but to share her people's fate, and tells of her leaving for the transit camp. And it tells of her life in the camp as she cared for the most vulnerable, and chronicled in graphic detail the story of their fate – a fate that she shared as she departed on the train to Auschwitz.

Finally, it reflects on the meaning and significance of her life and spirituality for us now, in our very different time.

It is an extraordinary story of an extraordinary human being whose life, in so short a time, was transformed; and who, although she did not survive the evil of the Holocaust, triumphed over it.

# Acknowledgements

I would like to thank the following who have helped and encouraged me in the writing of this book.

*In the Netherlands and Belgium*:
Professor Dr Klaas A. D. Smelik, Director of the Etty Hillesum Research Centre at Ghent University, who led the team which produced the book *Etty: The Letters and Diaries of Etty Hillesum 1941–1943*, for his support and encouragement.

The staff of the Jewish Historical Museum in Amsterdam, for their help in providing photographs from their archive, and allowing access to the diaries.

Frits Grimmelikhuizen, Founder of the Etty Hillesum Centre in Deventer, for his welcome, and for sharing further information about the Hillesum family in Deventer.

Judith Roosenschoon, Co-ordinator of the Etty Hillesum Centre in Deventer, for her welcome to the Centre.

*In the UK*:
All who have attended workshops or seminars on Etty Hillesum that I have led, who, by their interest and enthusiasm, have encouraged me to write in order to make her story more widely known.

Colleagues in the Chapter of Wells Cathedral, for their support and enabling me to take a period of study leave.

Charles and Hilary Cain, and Sarah Hargreaves, for their kindness and generosity in providing quiet places in which to write.

Elsa van der Zee, for her care and help in translating texts from the original Dutch, especially a particular diary entry mentioned in Chapter 4; and the letter, so far only available in Dutch, mentioned at the end of Chapter 6.

John Clarke, Dean of Wells, for his interest and encouragement from the beginning, and for help in commenting on drafts of each of the chapters of the book.

Peter Lippiett, Spirituality Adviser in the Portsmouth Diocese, for his support and help in commenting on a draft of the entire book.

Finally, my biggest debt of gratitude is to my wife Sam, for her constant encouragement, perceptive wisdom and support throughout the whole process.

# Who Was Etty Hillesum?

## *A brief summary of her life*

Etty Hillesum was born on 15th January 1914 in the town of Middelburg in Holland where her father, Dr Louis Hillesum, taught classical languages. After moves to Hilversum, Tiel and Winschoten, in 1924 the family moved to Deventer, a medium-sized city in the east of Holland where Louis was appointed assistant headmaster, and then in 1928 headmaster of the local Gymnasium. Here Etty grew up. Her father came from a Dutch Jewish family, while her mother Riva (Rebecca Bernstein) was Russian by birth and had fled to the Netherlands after a pogrom in Russia. Etty had two younger brothers, Jacob (Jaap) born in 1916, and Michael (Mischa) born in 1920. They were both brilliant in their different fields – Jaap in medicine and Mischa in music – but both suffered from serious mental illness and spent time in psychiatric institutions.

In 1932, Etty left her father's school and went to Amsterdam to study law. She went on to study Slavic languages at Amsterdam and Leiden, and continued to study Russian during the period of her diaries, and had a number of private pupils. During her university years she was involved in 'left-wing antifascist student circles and was politically and socially aware without belonging to a political party'.[1]

In March 1937 she took a room at 6 Gabriël Metsustraat in south Amsterdam in the house of an accountant Hendrik (Han) Wegerif, a widower aged 62 who hired her as a housekeeper. He also began an affair with her. She lived in this house until her final departure for Westerbork in 1943, and it was in her room there that much of her diary was written. The small community of people who shared the house with her were important to her. In addition to Han Wegerif there was his 21-year-old son Hans, a German cook named Käthe, a student Bernard Meylink, and a nurse, Maria Tuinzing, who became one of Etty's close friends.

The most important relationship of the diary is with the psycho-chirologist, Julius Spier. Born in 1887 in Germany, he had come to Amsterdam in 1939. Spier had worked in Zurich with Jung, who had encouraged him to develop his skill in chirology, the practice of psychoanalysis through the reading of people's palms. He was a gifted and charismatic figure and gathered around him a group of students, particularly women. Etty became part of this group and went into therapy with Spier, developing a close relationship with him and becoming his secretary.

The diary began – probably at Spier's suggestion – in March 1941 when Etty was just 27 years old. At the time Holland, which had capitulated to the Germans in May 1940, was increasingly under the Nazi reign of terror, and the Dutch Jews were beginning to be savagely persecuted.

The persecution gradually increased in severity through 1941 and 1942, and on 14th July 1942, at the instigation of her brother Jaap, Etty applied for a job at the Jewish Council and was appointed to do secretarial work. The Council was set up under the Nazis to deal with Jewish affairs. It believed that by negotiation it could mitigate the worst of the persecution. Etty disliked the work and on 30th July she was transferred at her own request to the department of 'Social Welfare for People in Transit' at Camp Westerbork.

Westerbork was a transit camp in the east of the Netherlands where the Nazis wanted to concentrate all the Dutch Jews, and from there over 100,000 went to their deaths in the extermination camps in the east. Working in the camp as a member of the Jewish Council, Etty was able to travel to Amsterdam and back on several occasions. Her first stay was to last – with the exception of one week – from the end of July 1942 to mid-September, a period of about six weeks.

Other than two weeks back at Westerbork in the late autumn, she spent the winter of 1942 and the spring of 1943 in Amsterdam because of illness. Eventually she was well enough to return to the camp, and on 6th June 1943 she left Amsterdam for Westerbork for the last time.

Her letters vividly describe the conditions of the camp at Westerbork: desperately overcrowded wooden barracks, labyrinths of barbed wire, watchtowers, mud and misery – in a patch of heath half a kilometre square. It was a community living in dread of the weekly transport which left each Tuesday with its freight wagons crammed full of men, women, children and infants bound for the east. In this hell she spent the last three months of her life caring for the vulnerable, visiting the sick in the hospital barracks, and writing letters to friends. By the person she was – by her vitality and warmth, her humanity and compassionate care – she became a source of life and inspiration to others. It was from this place that, despite everything that was happening around her, she wrote, 'life is glorious and magnificent'.

The last we know of her was the day she too, together with her parents and her brother Mischa, were deported on a train bound for Poland. The journey was to last three days. Before they finally left the Netherlands, Etty threw a postcard addressed to a friend out of the train. It was found and sent on by some farmers. It read: 'We left the camp singing.' They reached Auschwitz on 10th September. She died there on 30th November.

The Hillesum family in 1931. From left to right: Etty, Rebecca Hillesum-Bernstein, Mischa, Jaap, Dr Louis Hillesum

*Collection Jewish Historical Museum, Amsterdam*

Julius Spier c. 1930

Etty c. 1937–8

# Chapter 1

# An Emerging Self

*My 'centre' is growing firmer by the day ... in the past I was nothing but a fluttering insecure little bird.*

Etty Hillesum did not emerge from adolescence as a balanced young person already well on the way to becoming a saintly figure. The early pages of the diary reveal an insecure, emotionally disturbed and sexually chaotic young woman struggling with a turbulent inner life which she cannot understand and which from time to time pitches her into deep depression.

On 8th March 1941, the day before the first entry in the diary, she wrote a letter to Julius Spier with whom she had only just begun to meet. The letter indicates how clearly she understands her own need. After telling him 'I experienced strong erotic feelings for you ... and at the same time a strong aversion', and writing of her 'utter loneliness', and her 'uncertainty' and her 'fear', she writes:

... a small slice of chaos was suddenly staring at me from deep down inside my soul. And when I had left you and was going back home, I wanted a car to run me over, and I thought, ah, well, I must be out of my mind, like the rest of my family ... But I know again now that I am not mad, *I simply need to do a lot of work on myself before I develop into an adult and a complete human being.*[1] (my italics)

This is where the remarkable story of Etty Hillesum must begin, the story of a vulnerable and insecure young woman who knew she badly needed help.

In her first diary entry dated the next day, she writes:

> All my life I have had the feeling that, for all my apparent self-reliance, if someone came along, took me by the hand and bothered about me, I would be only too willing and eager to deliver myself up to his care. And there he was now, this complete stranger, this S. with his complicated face.[2]

Her tone is simple and childlike but apposite, for anyone who goes into therapy and is prepared to be open to what may be revealed will rapidly find themselves getting in touch with their inner child, with the story of their origins, with what their childhood has meant to them – *and with what it has done to them.*

## A disturbed family

It is clear that Etty Hillesum came from a deeply disturbed family. At various points in the diary she uses different words to describe her home – 'degenerate', 'tainted', a 'madhouse' – but the word most frequently used to sum up the confusion and shapelessness of it all, is 'chaos'. The roots of this chaos may be traced back to the problems and difficulties of her parents, to the stark incompatibility of their characters and the sharp contrast of their backgrounds, and what she later describes as their psychological and emotional inadequacy. They were simply, she writes, 'out of their depth'.[3]

Her father Louis was a quiet, shy and scholarly man who found it difficult to cope in the world. His shyness was made worse by the fact that he suffered from impaired vision, and deafness in one ear. Indeed, so poor was his vision that it is said that when he was headmaster in Deventer, the school caretaker used to bring him to and from the school every day. Born in Amsterdam in 1880, he was the fourth child of a Jewish merchant and the grandson of a Rabbi who had been Chief Rabbi in the north of the Netherlands, and so his background and upbringing were very much as a Dutch Jew.

His great strength was his intellect. He studied classics at Amsterdam University where he gained a bachelor and a masters degree, both '*cum laude*', and in 1911 he began his career teaching classics in Middleburg. However, though an excellent teacher, he had great difficulty keeping order in the classroom, particularly among younger pupils, and he would react to their unruly behaviour by becoming very strict. But he was a warm and cordial man and, though he found life beyond the world of books difficult, he had a wry sense of humour. As one of Deventer's leading citizens, he was widely appreciated for his cultural interests.

Etty's mother, Riva (Rebecca) Bernstein, could not have been more different. Chaotic, extravert and noisy, she was given to sudden emotional outbursts. With her curly red hair and strange Dutch accent she would have stood out in the streets of the small provincial city of Deventer. She had come to Holland in 1907, the first of her family to flee from the town of Surash in Tjernigol in Russia as a result of Jewish persecution. Dressed in the uniform of a soldier with her head shaved, she had arrived in Amsterdam in February 1907 and had begun to make her way in this new and very different country by teaching Russian. Her family soon followed her, first her brother Jacob and then her parents, but they stayed in Amsterdam for only a few years. After Riva and Louis were married in December 1912, the whole Bernstein family – her parents and her brother Jacob and his new wife and young child – emigrated illegally to the United States, leaving Riva behind to cope as best she could alongside her withdrawn and scholarly Dutch husband.

Being the first child of this unusual union, Etty may well have borne the brunt of their stormy marriage and the emotional confusion of a home life which her parents somehow simply did not know how to create. But her two brilliant younger brothers – Jaap who went on to study medicine, and Mischa who was exceptionally gifted in music – suffered too. Jaap was admitted to psychiatric hospitals on several occasions; and Mischa who became psychotic at the age of 16 was treated for schizophrenia, and right up to the end of his short life he was an insecure and psychologically fragile young man. Though he was a remarkably gifted young pianist, and in demand to perform across the country, Etty records how he 'simply refuses to play if they (his parents) are not there . . . In the past they used to visit mental hospitals and doctors, now they attend his concerts.'[4]

The mental illness of her brothers had a profound effect on Etty. Several diary entries indicate that the fear of mental illness lurked at the back of her mind. She saw her 'tainted family' as 'riddled with hereditary disease' and, at one of the darkest moments of the diary, she uses this to justify to herself her decision personally to abort her own child. She recalls a time in her home 'when Mischa got so confused and had to be carried off to an institution by force and I was witness to the whole horror of it, I swore to myself then that no such unhappy human being would ever spring from my womb'.[5]

## The family home

We gain a glimpse into the actual experience of her life as a child in the family home at Deventer when, in August 1941, just five months after she had begun her therapy with Julius Spier, she goes back and spends a week there.

On her second morning she finds herself remembering how it used to be: 'I always used to go to pieces in this madhouse. Nowadays I keep everything inwardly at arm's length and try to escape unscathed . . . it is as if every bit of energy were being sucked out of me.'[6]

On Sunday morning two days later, writing to Spier, she despairs over her home: 'Sometimes one feels so sad and heavy-hearted because of it all. In the past my picturesque family would cost me a bucket of desperate tears every night.' Aware of the depth of the disturbance both within her and all around her in this house, she adds:

'I can't explain these tears as yet; they come from somewhere in the dark collective unconscious.'[7]

A few days later, she continues:

I don't know what is the matter with this place, but one simply can't live here. For a week I managed to battle through splendidly, but suddenly I noticed that I was completely exhausted and incredibly unhappy. It feels as if my joie de vivre were constantly being whittled down in these surroundings, I no longer know how to defend myself here, it is as if great big stones were hanging from every part of my body, from my arms, from my legs, from my brain and from my heart, trying to drag me down into some kind of morass.[8]

Probably referring to outbursts from her mother, she tells him: 'In my dreams it is like the Wailing Wall in Jerusalem. I never remember anything definite when I wake up, all I know is that there has been a lot of heavy sighing and piteous sobbing.' After more complaints of her exhaustion and constant bad headaches, she relates how,

A few days ago, very early one morning when everyone was still asleep my younger brother ran away. He left a fairly pathetic but perfectly logical letter in which he wrote that he could no longer bear the atmosphere at home, that he refused to be sucked dry and that from now on he would live his own life. After a few days of searching . . . we discovered that he was with acquaintances in the country who had been kind enough to take him in. He doesn't want to come back home.

She finishes this little story with an emphatic flourish: 'How right he is, that young man!'

It is a bleak picture made all the more so because she is not blind to the potential riches that her parents, through their backgrounds, learning and cultural inheritance, have to offer:

Our house is a remarkable mixture of barbarism and culture. Spiritual riches lie within grasp but they are left unused and unguarded, carelessly scattered about. It is depressing, it is tragicomic. I don't know what kind of madhouse this really is, but I know that no human being can flourish here.[9]

'*I don't know what kind of madhouse this really is . . .*' As she writes this in August 1941, she does not understand it. However, over the months of her work with Spier, understanding does slowly begin to dawn. Towards the end of a long entry of 29th December, after nine months of working with him, she writes: 'I am beginning to understand something about my youth, about those recurring headaches and lethargic spells lasting for weeks on end, succumbing to the chaos within.'[10]

## Chaos

Before we look briefly at how this 'chaos' manifested itself in her, and how with Spier and others she began to deal with it, it is worth asking more precisely – what exactly was it? Where did it come from? And how, initially, did she try to comprehend it?

Of her two parents it is her mother whom she finds the most difficult. Throughout the diary, and even to the very end (by which time her relationship with them both has undergone radical change and she is able to care for them in the transit camp with great tenderness and affection), one senses that she is always closer to her father. Despite the anguish of these early diary entries, and later her embarrassment and confusion at his presence when he turns up in Amsterdam, her fondness for him – 'my little Papa'[11] – is never far below the surface. This preference is not surprising, for though she inherits from him his love of literature and intellectual giftedness, she is in fact very different from him. Temperamentally she takes after her hot-blooded Russian mother. It was doubtless because of her mother that she developed a passion for all things Russian – its language, literature and landscapes – but she found her mother's emotional turbulence very difficult to cope with, for in it she saw a reflection of her own budding confusion. So she felt a profound 'unresolved antipathy'[12] for her. In one entry she writes with great emphasis: 'Mother is a model of what I must never become.'[13]

The picture she paints of her is of an excitable but empty person whose moods vacillate wildly between 'forced vitality' and complaining exhaustion. She does not seem able to contain her mental disorganization and misery which spreads through her household like a contagion 'spoiling the atmosphere', draining the place of life, and no doubt producing a great deal of conflict. As Etty writes her August diary upstairs in her bedroom, she pauses at one point to add, 'Downstairs they are screaming blue murder with Father yelling, "Go then!" and slamming the door.'[14]

She also sees her mother as a profoundly needy person. She remembers how she once watched her eating at some function:

> She revolted me, sitting there, and at the same time I was filled with incredible pity for her. I really can't explain it. Her gluttony gave her the air of being terrified of missing out on anything. There was something terribly pathetic about her as well as something bestially repulsive . . . If I could only fathom what I really felt deep down, why I observed her so closely, then I would understand a great deal about my mother.[15]

In her father, she comes to see a lovable, but also a 'pathetic' figure, who has 'traded all his uncertainties, doubts, and probably also his physical inferiority complex, his insurmountable marriage problems, for philosophical ideas that . . . are totally vague. Those ideas help him to gloss over everything . . .'

Hidden behind his books, he surrenders to a kind of uncomprehending despair about life which he sees as 'chaos'. Etty finds this very threatening:

Beneath the surface, his resigned philosophy simply means: Oh well, which of us knows anything, all is chaos within and without. And it is that very chaos that also threatens me, that I must make my life's task to shake off instead of reverting to it time and again.[16]

At the heart of this family created by these two people there appears to be a void, a kind of muddled chaotic emptiness. Her parents are consumed with different kinds of anxiety, or in the case of her father, simply avoid life. There appears to be no strength or sense of presence. And so there can be no meeting of persons. All are left alienated and alone and somehow survive in their own isolation, confusion and anger. The family portrait taken in 1931 speaks volumes. It is cold and emotionally frozen. Nobody smiles. To one side – on the edge – is father withdrawn in his chair. At the back stands the distant figure of the older brother Jaap whom at several points in the diary Etty reports as being aggressive towards her. In the centre sits the large and rather strange-looking figure of the mother, with the gifted younger son Mischa beside her, his arm around her neck. He was perhaps the most disturbed of them all. To the right is Etty, her face utterly dead and devoid of any expression. Other than the arm of the younger son around the neck of his mother, there is no trace anywhere of any warmth. No sense of the personal – of human beings relating to one another.

In a diary entry of 24th April 1942, Etty remembers sitting 'at about the age of fifteen' in her father's small study, which she describes as 'untidy and impersonal as were all the rooms in all the different houses in which we ever lived . . .'[17] '*Impersonal.*' Perhaps this word gives the clearest clue to this family's confusion. It suggests that the houses in which they lived were never places with a sense of *personal belonging* which enabled them to meet and share together. In other words, her parents had not been able to create a 'home'.

Etty came to realize – with a sense of compassion – that, though gifted, her parents were emotionally inadequate people who simply could not cope with life. The profound differences in their cultural backgrounds, their incompatible temperaments, their personality problems and their resulting marital conflicts must all have played a part. They were not equipped for the challenging task of bringing up such gifted children. She writes:

> I think my parents always felt out of their depth and as life became more and more difficult they were gradually so over-whelmed that they became quite incapable of making up their minds about anything. They gave us children too much freedom of action, and offered us nothing to cling to. That was because they never established a foothold for themselves. And the reason why they did so little to guard our steps was that they themselves had lost the way.[18]

## A very troubled young woman

When she arrived for her first meeting with Julius Spier, this chaos of her dysfunctional family was part of the baggage that Etty carried within her. And she was a very troubled young woman. In the period after she had left home and come to live in Amsterdam as a student, she had moved restlessly from one set of lodgings to another until she settled in the house of Han Wegerif.

During this time her tempestuous needs and insecurity drove her into turbulent sexual relationships. Etty was very aware of herself as a highly erotic young woman with a vivid sexual imagination. 'If someone makes an impression on me,' she writes, 'I can revel in erotic fantasies for days and nights on end.'[19] And she saw herself as an 'accomplished' lover. In her first entry in the diary – 9 March 1941 – she had written, 'I am accomplished in bed, just about seasoned enough . . . to be counted among the better lovers . . .'[20]

But though 'accomplished', she also knew that much of her youth-ful sexual activity was born out of a kind of desperate need and had about it a feverish and destructive quality. In a diary entry of 12th

March 1942, a full year after she had begun meeting with Spier, she writes of meeting up again with one of her former lovers, a man named Max. He tells her that something in her has changed, '. . . you have turned into a real woman . . . your features, your gestures, they're as lively and expressive as ever, but now there's so much more wisdom . . .' She reflects later: '. . . it was the body of this man, who now walked beside me like a brother, to which I had once clung in terrible despair. That, somehow, was the most gladdening thing: something had survived . . . the revival of memories that no longer haunted us, *who once had lived so destructively off each other*'[21] (my italics).

How did this transformation, noticed by her former lover – this growth into 'a real woman' with the emergence in her of 'wisdom' (which in the Hebrew tradition represents the feminine aspect of the Divine) – how did it begin?

## Julius Spier – and a new home

It began through her meeting with Julius Spier. But Spier was not the only one who played a significant part. When, in 1937, Etty moved into the house of the 62-year-old widower Han Wegerif, she became part of a new home, very different from the one she had left, and through her friendships with those who shared the house she became part of a warm human community.

It is easy to underestimate the part that Han Wegerif played in her story. He is a gentle, tolerant and undemanding figure in the background of the diary, and with him Etty felt deeply 'at home'. He did not attempt to comprehend her difficulties, or respond to her powerful intellectual needs, but he gave her affection and sexual intimacy. But while she belonged to him, rather like a comfortable married couple, it was Spier who excited her and held out to her the possibility of life – and freedom from her confusions.

Spier's charismatic personality attracted round him many admirers, many of them young women. Etty's relationship with him developed in the context of this wider circle. Among those who were especially important to her were Henny Tideman whose simple faith played a part in her spiritual search, Dicky de Jonge the youngest of the Spier circle, Adri Holm, and the Zionist couple Werner and Liesl Levie. All these belonged to the group which gathered round Spier for intellectual discussion and musical evenings.

So as the barbarism of Nazi race hatred grew ever uglier around them, there grew up in Amsterdam this small community of intellectual life and spiritual nourishment – and Etty was at the heart of it. All these people played a part in her story, including too those who came to her for lessons in Russian. But it was the very personal relationship that developed between her and Spier – with all its shades of light and dark – that was the key to unlocking her future.

## A strange therapeutic relationship

As a *therapeutic* relationship it was highly unusual – a long way from any conventional idea of therapy such as we might expect today with clear understandings of professional boundaries and roles. And it went a great deal further. Indeed, the terms 'therapist' and 'patient' do not begin to describe the rich, complex and intimate friendship she made with this charismatic older man to whom she was attracted, and with whom she spiritually and literally struggled.

Julius Spier was a 'psycho-chirologist'. Born in Frankfurt in 1887, he had left a successful career in business to develop his interest in chirology – the reading of people's personalities through the study of their hands. In this he was encouraged by the great Swiss psychoanalyst Carl Jung with whom Spier spent two years in apprentice analysis. Jung wrote the introduction to Spier's book *The Hands of Children,* which explains the basic principles of chirology, and the influence of Jung can be seen in Spier's thinking and approach. It was at Jung's recommendation that Spier opened a practice as a psycho-chirologist in Berlin in 1929, which was highly successful.

However, in his domestic life things were not so straightforward. In 1934 Spier divorced his wife Hedl Rocco, and after several affairs he became engaged to one of his students, Hertha Levi, who became his secretary. She emigrated to London around 1938, but right up to his death from cancer in 1942, Spier was in touch with her. They corresponded regularly and he was concerned to try to remain faithful to her. He died with her name on his lips.

In 1939 Spier received permission to emigrate to the Netherlands after payment of a large amount of money to the Nazis, and he arrived in Amsterdam in January of that year and stayed with his sister for the first few months until he found lodgings in south Amsterdam, not far from where Etty was living.

Spier began his teaching and therapeutic relationships with the many young women who came to him, by reading their palms. This was how Etty first met him. She was invited to his rooms in Amsterdam as a 'model' at one of his courses where he taught palm-reading. But the focus did not stay for long simply on the hands. In one of her very early sessions with him he encouraged her to wrestle with him, and it would seem that wrestling became an occasional part of their early relationship. Spier was a big man and one can only imagine his surprise and consternation when, on the first occasion they wrestled, this small young woman whom he hardly knew, threw him. Etty comments: 'All my inner tensions, the bottled-up forces, broke free, and there he lay, physically and also mentally, as he told me later, thrown. No one had ever been able to do that to him before, and he could not conceive how I had managed it.'[22] To the modern ear this all sounds highly questionable and, to say the least, irregular. However, in the climate of the interwar years – a period of bizarre psychoanalytical experimentation – it may not have been so unusual. Interestingly, there was at this time 'a popular movement in psychoanalysis, which proposed that a therapeutic relationship could only arise from a physical bond'.[23] Spier used to justify the wrestling by saying, 'body and soul are one'.[24]

Unusual or not, from the beginning Etty 'fell under the spell of the inner freedom that seemed to emanate from him'; she was excited by the possibilities of working with him, and was ready to

yield herself to him 'unreservedly'.[25] It was to be a risky and dangerous surrender.

Etty Hillesum was an intensely alive and sexual young woman, yet
she felt herself plagued by what she called her 'confounded eroti-
cism'.[26] This she saw clearly mirrored in Spier. Alarmingly, her first
meetings with him vividly awakened in her all the energies and
appetites that in the past had betrayed her so deeply and torn her
apart and which needed now not to be indulged but disciplined and
directed towards the finding of a deeper and fuller humanity. So he
seemed to offer her both hope, as a therapist, but disaster, as a man.

## A growing and deepening bond

However, because Etty trusted Spier and valued his evident gifts of
insight and analytical wisdom, and because she was ruthlessly determined 'to come to grips with myself',[27] over a long period she was,
despite her worst self, able to accomplish this disciplining and re-
directing of her energies. Their increasingly intimate friendship,
which was carried on at every level – intellectual, emotional, spiritual
and physical – spelt hope for her. First she was his pupil, then his
secretary, and eventually from time to time, his lover. Entry after
entry in her diary speaks of a growing and deepening bond, though
it was not all plain sailing.

For the first few months her feelings for him and about him are
tempestuous and frequently contradictory. Often she is consumed by
desire and longs for an affair with him; just now and then she longs to
be free of him; occasionally she feels used by him; often she finds
herself jealous of his relationship with others; just occasionally she
declares she is sick of him; and frequently she says how much she loves
and adores him. As the relationship develops, sometimes she finds
herself longing 'more for the human being than for the man'.[28] It was
an emotional roller-coaster, but despite the ups and downs and the
violent pulls of her passionate nature, overall hugely positive. Spier
gave her the emotional security, the intellectual stimulus and the

psychological insight which she so badly needed. 'What I am looking for', she writes in one entry, 'is my own truth'.[29] Spier helped her find it.

## A dark place

But this journey in search of her own 'truth', her own *identity*, which she pursued with extraordinary courage and honesty, took her into the depths of a profound personal struggle.

And she began from a dark place.

In the first diary entry of 9th March 1941 she writes how 'deep down something like a tightly wound ball of twine binds me relentlessly', and she condemns herself: 'at times I am nothing more or less than a miserable, frightened creature despite the clarity with which I can express myself'. She refers to her 'inner chaos' and to 'forces now at loggerheads within me', and her 'depression', and towards the end she writes of 'a really bad fit of depression, an inescapable pressure in my skull and gloomy thoughts, much too gloomy to bear for long . . .'[30]

In the next entry, we come across one of her many bouts of self-criticism. She finishes a long passage about her dreams as a writer by telling herself that she is, despite all her extravagant and romantic imagination, no more than 'a weakling and a nonentity adrift and tossed by the waves'.[31] Two days later she writes in the same vein: 'In near ecstatic moments I think myself capable of God knows what, only to sink back again into the deepest pit of uncertainty'.[32]

On 23rd March, having begun to emerge from her deep 'pit of uncertainty', and after a period of new confidence and vitality, she writes, 'Everything has gone wrong again, I long for something and don't know what it is. Inside I am totally at a loss, restless, driven, and my head feels close to bursting again.' In the same entry she writes of how 'last night . . . the turbulence began to swirl up inside me, as vapour swirls up from a swamp'. A few lines further on she adds, '. . . right now I am sunk in the mire'. And she ends, 'I hate myself like poison, and that's all there is to it!'[33]

It is a bleak picture, which reveals the depth of her need. There are many entries in the same vein. Bouts of depression threaten her through much of the early part of the diary. But it is not all dark. There are times when she sees new possibilities, and believes things have really changed, but as she finds hope and despair alternating within her, it is a fragile confidence.

On 12th March she asks: 'Has a new phase of my life really begun?'[34] Five days later she writes, '. . . I sensed my new inner strength for the first time . . .';[35] on 19th March, she is confident that what has plagued her past is beginning to be dealt with: '. . . my inner forces have been concentrated, they have started to fight against my appetite for adventure and my far ranging erotic curiosity'.[36] The next morning she is excited by the sense of a longer view of her life stretching out ahead of her: 'Very early this morning, suddenly that distant horizon: your whole life lies before you, *you are only just starting to live*'[37] (my italics). On 24th March 1941 she exclaims: 'When I am well I have absolutely nothing in common with the person I am when I am not well . . . now I am brimming again with hope and strength and a genuine zest for life . . . I have once more moved on . . . much surer of myself . . .'[38]

But only the day before – the 23rd – she had been 'totally at a loss'.

Through the summer and autumn, despite times of calm and growing strength, the underlying self-doubt persists, and her depressions continue to plague her. 8th May: '. . . everything has ground to a halt . . . depressed'; 8th June: '. . . a mass of uncertainties still at large'; 4th July: '. . . each day . . . a thousand fragments'; 7th August: '. . . would like to disappear . . . to forget and be rid of myself'; 4th September: '. . . heart once again frozen . . . brain squeezed by a large vice.' 25th September: '. . . the germs of the crises are always there'; 5th October: 'I feel too awful for words . . . as dismal and depressed as can be'; 12th October: '. . . the best thing would be to go and throw myself into a canal'. And the entry of 30th October sums up the depth of the pit that again and again she finds herself falling into: 'Mortal fear in every fibre. Complete collapse. Lack of self-confidence. Aversion. Panic.'[39]

## Temperament and context

There were two factors that particularly contributed to the violence of this psychological roller-coaster ride.

First, her temperament. Etty Hillesum was not only a highly intelligent young woman, but also an unusually intense personality, living life with an exhausting passion. This was crucial in helping to make her who she became. It gave her the energy that drove her on in her self-exploration and the ruthless determination to deal with what she did not like; and it contributed to her eventual greatness. But there is a price to be paid for exploring and experiencing life in such a total and demanding way. Frequently she was exhausted through the violence of her mood swings. And so before she learnt how 'to stop and listen to myself' – to 'sound my own depths'; before she found 'a basic tune, a steady undercurrent',[40] and so was able to harness the immensely powerful forces within her, the result was often emotional chaos.

A second and crucial factor was her context. Everything in the diary and letters is set against the background of the Nazi terror sweeping across Europe. Its horror is never far away, it darkens everything and questions whether human life within its terrible shadow can have any meaning. On 14th June she writes: 'More arrests, more terror, concentration camps, the arbitrary dragging off of fathers, sisters, brothers. We seek the meaning of life, wondering whether any meaning can be left.'[41] Her own private struggle is therefore inextricably intertwined with an inferno of hatred and fear raging around her. The effect of this darkening nightmare on individual members of the Jewish race is impossible for us now to fully grasp. Etty was eventually to triumph over the power of this fear, but no one could escape entirely unscarred from the effects of such universal terror.

## A luminous figure

The personal turbulence of this young woman is very evident in the early part of the diary. What is astonishing is that in just two years –

despite all that was happening around her – she succeeded in breaking through to an altogether deeper dimension of living. She went on to explore and develop an inner life of such depth and richness that not only was she sustained through the hell of the transit camp, but she became a luminous figure to those who knew her and for whom she cared in the camp. She was a vital, life-giving presence in the midst of darkness and evil. It was a triumph of the human spirit, the foundations of which lay buried deep within her chaotic heart and which it would take time, through her relationship with Julius Spier, to uncover.

## A relationship of many dimensions

As the modern reader gets caught up in this first part of Etty Hillesum's story – and particularly the detail of the relationship with Spier with its sweaty bouts of wrestling, its sexual intimacies easily taken, and the huge disparity of age and life situations between this therapist and his patient, she or he may feel ill at ease. Certainly what happened between them was neither conventional nor what we today would regard as acceptable. But for her it was not just immensely positive, but life saving. As her relationship with him grew and developed, it became far more than simply 'therapy'. A rich multifaceted friendship flowered between them which embraced far more than just psychological understanding, crucial though that was.

Initially the relationship *is* simply therapist and patient. Right at the beginning he helps her place her depressions in context. 'He assigned their proper places to all the things that went on inside me,' she writes, 'it was like a jigsaw puzzle, all the pieces were mixed up, and he put them together properly.'[42]

Often it is teacher and pupil. He shares with her enquiring mind the range of his wide knowledge and experience in psychotherapy and his understanding of Jung and the emerging psychoanalytical tradition. On one occasion she writes to him, 'You, my beloved . . . priceless, private, psychological university. I have so much to discuss with you again and so much to learn from you.'[43]

Frequently she is the child and he is the parent. Several times she describes herself as curling up childlike at his feet, resting against his legs. There is no doubt that as well as a longed-for lover, Spier was also the strong and intimately caring father that she had never had.

More and more, as their friendship deepens, they become intellectual soul-mates. She pedals back from his flat – just five streets, one bridge and one canal away – and they are on the phone again discussing Jung's *Symbols of Transformation* . . . reflecting on Rilke's letters . . .

Sometimes he is the sensual man excited by her, the erotic young woman – and both of them struggle with the power of their desire, he constrained by his commitment to his fiancée in London, she constrained by her loyalty to 'Pa Han', the other older man in her life.

Occasionally she is the disappointed young woman threatened by doubt coping with cold responses from the professional man pre-occupied with other things. 'He has been so busy these last few days. It feels just as if he had abandoned me in his thoughts, so distant has he been . . . now I simply tell myself, so be it, it is ebb-tide . . .'[44]

From time to time, as we shall see in the next chapter, he is the believer in God and reader of the New Testament who prays and meditates and is deeply positive about religion, who slowly and hesitantly shares his faith and practice with her, a sceptical and searching young woman hungry for deeper meaning.

In the later stages, he is the practitioner of wisdom and analytical care, and she the budding apprentice, as she begins to take on her own people whom she sees for therapy.

And just now and then, they are two vulnerable human beings together, oblivious of age and in love, determined to be carefree in the terrible times in which they live, laughing and playing and discovering through each other their own inner playful child, and, against the ever-menacing backdrop of the violence and the restrictions, experiencing *delight*.

I was still chuckling out on the street . . . We managed with great difficulty to get three lemons from a barrow, by paying ten cents apiece instead of the usual seven. But we were determined to have some cake and whipped cream. And then we roamed the streets again, I hanging playfully onto his arm with my Cossack hat askew on my head and he with a silly-looking alpine cap above his grey mane, like two crazy lovers.[45]

## The secret

Perhaps the most remarkable thing about this rich tapestry of an ever more intimate and trusting friendship which they wove together was how rapidly it grew – just 18 months, from March 1941 to September 1942. But they knew that their time was very short. And can we pinpoint the secret of it all?

Among the huge amount that Etty wrote in her diary about Spier, two sentences stand out which point to the heart of the matter – what it was about this relationship that was for her so liberating and life-giving.

On 10th August 1941, while staying with her parents at her home in Deventer, she wrote to him: 'You are, in fact, the first person to whom I have ever related inwardly . . .'[46] And on 1st December 1941 she wrote in her diary: '. . . by coming into such very close contact with him over and over again, something is happening to me . . . he is the unyielding rock and my moods lap around him.'[47]

'You are, in fact, the first person to whom I have ever related inwardly.'

'He is the unyielding rock and my moods lap around him.'

These two sentences sum up the essence of what Spier meant to her. Through his skill, his powers of perception and his capacity for deep empathetic understanding, he enabled her to open up her chaotic heart. In her confusion, she felt herself understood and accepted by another human being, *for the first time in her life*. As he went on accepting and absorbing the depths and heights of her mood-swings, his strength and dependability enabled her to accept them also, and so to integrate what before she had been unable to cope with.

For the first time in her life she related *authentically* – in her vulnerability, need and strength – to another person. His affirmation of her enabled her to belong to herself, so that she began to be at peace in the world, no longer driven by her compulsions and needs. She was becoming whole.

## A bedrock

Towards the end of the first year of meeting with him, she begins to touch a bedrock within. The dominant note is growing confidence. Something is happening in her. On 29th December she writes: 'We can steer by what has taken shape in us, by what has reached our consciousness from the deepest depths and has then taken shape.'[48] She tells of a visit back again to her parents' home in Deventer, but this time waking up and 'revelling in the day so brave and fresh, feeling the sharp contours of your own self'. She goes on to say the chaos can still overwhelm her at times, 'as if I were on a great grey ocean', (in the biblical tradition the ocean is often the symbol of chaos) 'but on the bottom *there are hills rising, elevations taking shape, the appearance of form*'[49] (my italics).

In this young woman a sense of self is slowly emerging from beneath the chaos of her psyche. A few weeks later she writes: 'I draw on an ever-deeper inner certainty . . . Time and again I have had to learn how spacious the heart can be, and time and again I have had to reclaim that space.'[50] Significantly, it is at this time that a religious sense is growing stronger within her.

One of the earliest signs of this emerging self is her discovery of the value of solitude. One evening back in August, she writes of walking alone through the darkened streets of Amsterdam:

Quite suddenly I had the impression that I wasn't alone, that there were two of us. I felt as if I consisted of two people who were squashed tightly together and felt so good and so warm as a result. I was in such close touch with myself, full of inner warmth, and felt utterly self-sufficient . . . I discovered with no small satisfaction that I got on very well with myself.[51]

Later, the need for solitude becomes fundamental to her. 'All of us', she writes, 'carry a vast and fruitful loneliness wherever we go . . . sometimes the most important thing in a whole day is the rest we take between two deep breaths.'[52]

As confidence grows, she finds too that she is able to absorb the negative without being overwhelmed by it; she discovers that sadness and joy are integral to one another and she can hold them both.

In the past – I feel more and more justified now in calling it the past as a lasting change seems to have set in with me – when I was in a bad mood or depressed, I would completely lose touch with my other self. And that no longer happens. Now I carry my sadness and my gladness and everything else with me all the time.[53]

And she discovers something else; the experience of being awake to the gift of the ever-new present moment, rather than, as in the past, hanging on to despair:

. . . one of my latest achievements: the realisation that every moment gives birth to a new moment, full of fresh potential, and sometimes like an unexpected present. And that one must not cling to moments of malaise and prolong them needlessly, because in so doing one may prevent the birth of a richer moment. Life courses through one as a constant current in a great series of moments . . .[54]

Gradually, over many weeks and months the diary reveals a young woman finding wholeness, discovering and appreciating her self, able to value solitude and absorb the negative without going under, and, freer of the worst of her compulsive needs, delighting in the present moment.

## A new birthday

As she breaks through onto this inner ground, it is all vividly, wonderfully new. On 3rd February 1942, the anniversary of her first meeting with Spier, she feels she has been born anew – that she is just one year old. In a letter to her friend Gera Bongers dated 6th February, she writes jauntily:

> Did you know that on Tuesday, 3rd February, I celebrated my first birthday? Because it was precisely one year ago, on February 3rd 1941, that I was brought into the world by an ogre of a man wearing green plus fours and an antenna on his head . . .[55]
> (a reference to his hearing aid)

In the diary she adds: 'I think I'll celebrate 3rd February as my birthday from now on – it is more important than 15th January, the day my umbilical cord was cut.'[56]

It is an astonishing change. She writes as though her previous life had not even existed, such is the delight in the new identity that is emerging slowly, falteringly, into the world. And though it was still very partial and there would be many future dark moments, it was also very real. Time, and the testing that was yet to come, would show that.

And the date of her new 'birthday' is the day she met Spier. He was at the heart of this first transformation in this story of many transformations. After his death seven months later in September, she writes of him as a kind of midwife to her very being – 'the one', she says with profound gratitude, 'who had attended at the birth of my soul'.[57]

## Letting go and a deeper dependency

Spier was crucial in this journey of self-discovery. With him she began and with him she grew. But there would be a final step she would need to take if she was really to know who she was and stand fully on her own two feet; and that would be to let go of him, on whom she had so deeply depended. This last and necessary stage of her relationship with him does eventually happen, though it is not until some time later, in the summer of 1942.

In July of that year Spier was ill with cancer and near the end, and Etty came to recognize that she could now forge her own future. As we shall see later, in Chapter 4, at this point in her diary the focus noticeably shifts. The horror of what is happening to the Jewish community moves from the sidelines of her writing to the forefront. It can no longer be kept on the margins, and she is ready to face it. As she turns to this wider, darker picture, references to her life with Spier change. Still they spend precious time together, but he grows steadily weaker, the balance of their relationship alters, and she breaks free of her dependency on him as her attention moves to what lies ahead.

By then, too, she has found a deeper dependency. This and this alone will sustain her through the coming storm.

But it needs to be said – for Spier remains a questionable figure – that without his skill in dealing with her through the vivid and intimate journey they travelled together through 1941 and the first half of 1942, and without the emerging spirituality and faith he encouraged her to explore, she would never have been able either to grow up or move on. Their extraordinary relationship enabled her original longing to be fulfilled. On 5th April 1942 she wrote: 'I only know that I love him, a bit more every day, and that I ripen beside him into a genuine and adult human being.'[58]

Over the months of her 'ripening', he gave her what she regarded as her most precious inheritance from him. On the night of his death she writes in her diary directly to him: 'What energies I possess have been set free inside me. You taught me to speak the name of God without embarrassment.'[59]

To that deeper dimension of her journey – and their relationship – we now turn.

Etty c. 1940
*Collection Jewish Historical Museum, Amsterdam*

# Chapter 2

# Discovering God

*The girl who could not kneel but learned to do so on the rough coconut matting in the untidy bathroom.*

The first part of Etty Hillesum's diary is a story of rescue and recovery. As the Nazi terror intensifies, this passionate young woman confronts and struggles with her disordered personality, and begins to find herself. It is a moving account of personal redemption. But if it had been the sum total of Etty's story, we would never have heard of her. Having brought some order to her inner chaos, it was her exploration into and beyond her self, her profoundly religious quest, which paved the way to her real greatness. It was this which enabled her in the midst of the horror of the Holocaust to retain her humanity, and to transform, even there in the camp, how the world can be *seen*.

Yet this further exploration was one for which she had no blueprint, no previous religious experience to call on. She had to forge her own way.

## No previous religious experience

As the diary begins, though she is of course a Jew, Etty shows no particular interest in religion in terms of observance. And that was simply what she had been used to. She had not been brought up with any religious commitment. Indeed, as we have seen, her parents made little attempt to shape their children's lives by any code or set of moral or religious guidelines. 'They . . . offered us nothing to cling to' she writes, '. . . because they never established a foothold for themselves.'[1]

Her father had an interest in Judaism, but it was the detached interest of a bookish scholar, not the practising interest of a believer. There was no observance behind it. In his introduction to her diary and letters, Klaas Smelik comments that 'although interested in Jewish identity, Hillesum was highly assimilated';[2] and the fact that not once in the diary does Etty ever mention synagogue attendance or Jewish family ritual confirms that there was no family tradition.

Her student years were marked by her restlessness, her sexual adventurism, her interest in left-wing politics, and by her love of learning, particularly in Slavic studies which she studied at Leiden under the guidance of the eccentric Professor Nicolas van Wijk whom she revered. Her intellectual curiosity and passion for books was a deep part of her life, and would have provided some counterbalance to her emotional confusions.

Life for a student in the 1930s would have been overshadowed by the rise of fascism with its brutal disrespect for learning, and by the sense of a world moving ominously towards war. She describes van Wijk's large house at Leiden as 'a small oasis of peace and refreshment and respect for learning',[3] and when in March 1941 she hears of his sudden death she is deeply shocked. 'I cannot describe the dismay I felt', she writes, 'on reading the unexpected news of van Wijk's death . . . it has made more of an impression on me than the whole war. It is almost a sinister symbol of the war, of the destruction of culture.'[4] She remembers other teachers whom she has admired who have also died or disappeared, or been sent to concentration camps, particularly Willem Bonger, the Professor of Criminology at Amsterdam whose lectures she had attended. She tells of how – just before the capitulation of Holland in May 1940 – she was the last person to speak to this courteous and 'broken' old man as she walked with him across a park. After she had taken her leave of him and he had gently bid her farewell, 'his hands between mine', he went home and she hears next day that 'he put a bullet through his brain at eight o'clock'.[5] Suddenly the brutality of war came terribly near.

One of the rich threads of her life with Julius Spier was the intellectual life they shared together. With him she explored her love of books and passion for learning. But as she entered into her personal struggle her outlook was by and large humanist, not formed by a religious framework of understanding. For the first few months of their relationship her thinking remained that way. In the early period of the diary, references to faith and belief are few and scattered.

As a psycho-chirologist, Spier would have worked within a largely humanist frame of reference. Over his time in Berlin he had developed 'chirology', a psychological theory which focused on the form and detail of the hands, though it was recognized that, even for a trained eye, this could not give the whole picture, and proper account needed to be given to other factors in the life of the individual. But it was a 'scientific' discipline, one area of development – albeit somewhat bizarre – in the still young movement of psychoanalytical study that was developing across Europe.

So as Etty went into her therapy with Spier, she had behind her an upbringing that had not been shaped by religious observance; and as she faced up to her need, she began to explore the insights of a largely 'secular' discipline. As far as we can discern, she was not particularly interested in the practice of religious faith, nor did she show any interest in any institutional expression of religion.

## The origins of faith

And so an important question: Where did the religious faith, which was to become so fundamental to who she became, come from? How did it make its first beginnings in her story? *What was its genesis?*

The first step towards what eventually became a deep religious faith was not through any interest in 'religion' as such at all. It was more to do with a sense in her of the inadequacy of the way that she, as an intellectual young woman educated in a modern university in post-Enlightenment Europe, engaged with the world around her – predominantly through the *mind*. It was to do with the limitations of conceptual understanding, of rationality itself.

Good though her mind was, as she learnt to analyse and categorize things, she found herself left with a feeling of alienation, and an inescapable sense of the human mind being too much at the centre of things 'subjecting' everything around it, through its powers of reason, to itself. Without quite knowing what she was doing, probably not even thinking consciously about it, she discovered within herself a need to find another, deeper way of response. Reason alone was not enough: something else was required. Not so much the response of the mind grasping and dealing with life through *thinking*, more the response of the heart simply attending to and receiving what *is*.

On 16th March 1941 – one month after she had begun to meet with Spier – she found herself taking, without really being aware of what was happening, a first tentative step on a new road – which would become her royal road. She tells of a moment one afternoon when she was sitting outside on the dustbin in the sun beside a chestnut tree. In the quiet of that moment she became aware of a step being taken in regard to how she was responding to what was around her. In the past she would have taken it all in with her mind. Now she finds herself – quite 'unconsciously' – bowing her head and simply 'receiving' what is there, in her heart. In this simple, spontaneous response, something happens. A step is taken, and there is a difference.

> Just now, when I was sitting on the dustbin in the sun out on our stony little terrace, with my head leaning against the washtub and with the sun on the strong, dark, still, leafless branches of the chestnut tree, I had a very clear sense of the difference between then and now . . . The sun on the dark branches, the chirping birds, and me on the dustbin in the sun.

In the past I would sit like that quite often too, but except for just once I had never before felt as I did this afternoon. In the past, I took in the tree and the sun with my intellect. I wanted to put down in so many words why I found it so beautiful, I wanted to understand how everything fitted together, I wanted to fathom that deep primitive feeling with my *mind* . . . In other words I wanted to subject nature, everything, to myself. I felt obliged to interpret it. *And the quite simple fact is that now I just let it happen to me . . . As I sat there like that in the sun, I bowed my head unconsciously as if to take in even more of that new feeling for life. Suddenly I knew deep down how someone can sink impetuously to his knees and find peace there, his face hidden in his folded hands.*[6] (my italics)

## A profound contemplative faculty

It is a significant moment. She becomes aware, perhaps for the first time, of a profound contemplative faculty within her. It was to shape the person she became.

And it is the beginning of a journey. But the first steps are wavering, unsure. A few days later, racked by tensions, she doubts her experience and could not understand how it had happened. '. . . I am a long way from that blessed feeling of "submitting" to things', she writes, 'I no longer understand how I could have felt like that last week, sitting so peacefully on the dustbin in the sun . . .'[7] But however fragile and momentary, an appetite had been kindled, a trail had been found. She had glimpsed what wholeness might mean – something to do with an 'unconscious' bowing of the head enabling her 'to take in' not an idea, but a feeling – for life.

Spier encouraged her in this contemplative approach. He believed that a religious life was important and he encouraged his pupils to take time every morning for withdrawal, for reflection, for listening. Etty referred to it as 'the Buddhist quarter of an hour'.[8]

Sunday the 8th June: I think that I'll do it anyway: I'll turn inward for half an hour each morning before work, and listen to my inner voice. Lose myself. You could also call it meditation. I am still a bit wary of that word. But anyway, why not? A quiet half-hour within yourself . . . But it's not so simple, that sort of 'quiet hour'. It has to be learned. A lot of unimportant inner litter and bits and pieces have to be swept out first. Even a small head can be piled high inside with irrelevant distractions. True, there may be edifying emotions and thoughts, too, but the clutter is ever present. So let this be the aim of meditation: to turn one's innermost being into a vast empty plain, with none of that treacherous undergrowth to impede the view. So that something of 'God' can enter you, and something of 'Love' too.[9]

In this diary entry the words 'God' and 'Love' are hedged around with inverted commas. At this stage in her journey, it is not just the word 'meditation' that needs to be treated with caution.

As, tentatively, she began to explore a new path, the fact that she had not grown up in a practising faith tradition, and had neither a language of religion to call upon nor a mental library of religious terms to borrow from that might have defined in its own terms what was happening to her, is a blessing. It meant that what became her faith was from the beginning rooted and grounded in her own immediate, personal and direct experience. She had nothing else.

As this new path was pursued, the direction was ever inward. She became more and more vividly aware of a separation between the thinking mind and the more hidden inner sources which she was in search of – between consciousness, and what lies deeper than consciousness.

## Not thinking but listening

On the morning of 10th June, with the zeal of a new convert she writes: 'Not thinking, but listening to what is going on inside you. If you do that for a while every morning . . . you acquire a kind of calm that illumines the whole day.'[10] On 5th September, the conviction has grown:

> Thinking gets you nowhere. It may be a fine and noble aid in academic studies, but you can't think your way out of emotional difficulties. That takes something altogether different. You have to make yourself passive then, and just listen. Re-establish contact with a slice of eternity.[11]

Late at night on 5th October she reflects:

> One day I shall surely strike a balance between thinking and feeling. But this is my remedy: do not speak, do not listen to the outside world, but be perfectly still, try letting your innermost being resound, and listen to that. It is the only way.[12]

Two days later she is still pondering this balance:

> You shouldn't live on your brains alone but on deeper, more abiding sources, though you should gratefully accept your brains as a precious tool for delving into what problems your soul brings forth.[13]

And on 27th October she writes: 'You must live and breathe with your soul . . . If you live by your mind alone, yours is but a poor existence.'[14]

She applies this new conviction specifically to psychological understanding. She remembers an occasion when two friends, Jan Bool who was actively involved in the resistance, and Leonie Snatager, a close friend, came to see Spier, and he 'reached straight into their hearts with his analysis'. She did not think this was satisfactory for he seems to have summed them up in terms of a 'psychological formula'. She reflects: '. . . I still think that people can't be reduced to psychological formulas, that only the artist can render human beings to their last irrational elements'.[15] '*Only the artist.*' Etty knew better than most that human beings can be profoundly 'irrational', driven and pulled by forces far deeper than mere reason can tame. She had seen it in her family, she knew it in her self. Only the healer who is also an artist, she was convinced, could adequately address such hidden sickness, the power of irrational elements, for art seeks insights from a level of consciousness deeper than that which merely repeats 'psychological formulas'. And art, of course, is very close to religion.

## Encouraged by Jung

In her enthusiasm for this new understanding, she knew she was on to something. And she was encouraged by her reading of Jung. As a young psychiatrist appointed in 1900 to the Burghölzli Clinic in Zurich, Jung had pioneered work on the unconscious, believing that paying careful attention to the hidden, irrational and strange unconscious material in his patients was the key to their healing. She was excited by his valuing of the neglected depths of the mind, from where dreams and images and intuition come, and she intuitively understood its importance. She wrote, '. . . there is a dream world and a grey everyday real world . . . and I do so want to reconcile them. I want to live them both at the same time.'[16]

## Spiritual imagination

She had a natural affinity for this, for she had an immensely fertile spiritual imagination. Indeed, it could be said that it was as much her spiritual imagination, her openness to the images arising from her *unconscious* mind, as much as her love of the words explored in her *conscious* mind that gave her life its spiritual foundation. She too was an artist – through her imagination.

At the beginning, as we have seen, the images which come to her are dark and threatening. She imagines 'a tightly wound ball of twine' binding her 'relentlessly'; she sees 'forces at loggerheads' within her; 'a small slice of chaos' stares up at her from deep within her soul; her turbulence seems to her to be like vapour swirling up from 'a swamp'.[17]

Gradually, though, chaos begins to give way to order, light begins to dawn, and she begins to imagine her inner world as being wide and clear and spacious. She writes: 'My inner landscape consists of great, wide plains, infinitely wide, with hardly a horizon in sight – one plain merging into the next. As I sit huddled up in this chair, my head bowed low, I roam across those bare plains . . .'[18] Just how much this sense of inner space was part of her is clear in a later diary entry made early one Sunday morning:

> What was it like this morning just before I woke up? An almost tangible feeling, just as if there were all sorts of spaces and dis-tances locked up inside me which now wanted to break out to unfold into ever wider spaces and distances. As if the distances were tangible things I had to let out. Like stamping and pawing horses from a crowded stable. That spatial feeling within me is very strong . . . As if infinite steppes lay spread out inside me – I can see them and feel them and move over them.[19]

Occasionally other images come to her – of rivers, fields, rooms and buildings – but she returns again and again to the plains, her imagination feeding on her romantic love of Russia. As this sense of an inner world grows, she is delighted, even surprised by it: 'that one should carry such an awe-inspiring space within oneself!', she exclaims in a kind of surprised astonishment, and she insists: 'the inner world is as real as the outer world . . . It too has its landscapes, contours, possibilities, its boundless regions.'[20]

## Soul-landscape

She gives this inner world a label: 'Soul-landscape'. One day on the train, returning to Deventer, she looks out of the window at the landscape passing by – the open skies, the waterways, the wide Dutch fields, and she reflects:

> ... it is as if I were riding through the landscape of my own soul. Soul-landscape. I feel like that often: that the outer landscape is the reflection of the inner. Thursday afternoon along the river IJssel. A radiant, sweeping, bright landscape. And a feeling as if I were travelling through my own soul.[21]

Later, reading Rilke authenticates her experience, and she eagerly copies him down: 'We project images from within us, we take every opportunity to be world-builders, we erect thing upon thing round our innermost being.'[22]

Her 'soul-landscape' was saving for her, though it was not always limited to the land. Landscapes and seascapes could vie with one another for her inner attention. One morning in a dreamlike state she sees herself like a boat gliding through the waves: 'I slip through the grey Ocean of Eternity like a narrow boat.'[23] And this is no mere day-dreaming. Her subconscious is creating an image which defines herself to herself, in terms of harmony and integration. It is saving. A few days later, threatened again by depression, she writes, 'Once again I have been ... redeemed by an image'; and she recalls how '... a few days ago the image of ... sailing like a ship through my year of days ... saved me from being torn apart and cast to the winds'. 'I find that ... all this analysing makes me ... more miserable still, while a sudden poetic image ... liberates me.'[24]

She has found a way, deeper than mere reason, of dealing with her turmoil. It helps save her from depression, plays its part on her journey towards integration, and opens up to her the inner ground of her life, so that she finds what is *deepest and best in me*.

This she begins to call 'God'.

## God

On 10th August 1941, five months after her first meeting with Spier, the word 'God', used in this way, occurs for the first time. How it appears seems at first almost casual but, if we read carefully, it is a moment of revelation. She has realized something profound, though she cannot really put it into words.

She is back at her parents' home in Deventer. She receives a letter from Spier. As she reads it, she at first feels 'alienated' and 'out of touch' with him and with herself. Then, she writes in her diary: '*I regained contact with myself, with the deepest and best in me, which I call God, and so also with you.*' In this moment of 'contact' there is a deep recognition of *inter-connectedness.* She writes: 'Many new perceptions about myself and my bond with you and my fellow beings appeared.' She uses an image to try, inadequately, to convey how important this moment is: '. . . that moment, so important for me, lies within me like a rounded and complete whole, but still I cannot find the words to set it all down.'[25]

'God', she says, is what is 'deepest and best in me.' And what is 'deepest and best' in her is her *belonging – her 'at-one-ness' with Spier, and all other human beings.*

In this identification of her truest and deepest self with 'God', she is echoing a profound strand in the mystical writers of many traditions. '. . . there is only one problem on which all my existence, my peace and my happiness depend,' wrote Thomas Merton from his monastery in Kentucky, 'to discover myself in discovering God. If I find Him I will find myself and if *I find my true self, I will find Him*'[26] (my italics).

For Merton also, the 'true self' did not mean the individual separate 'me', the ego, but human beings *in communion, across all boundaries.* His life, his writings, his travelling to the East was spent in service of that conviction, that vision. Like Merton, Etty too was to become a universal person, seeking to be in communion with all peoples across all boundaries.

## Hearkening

But she was only just beginning on this road. As she begins to sense her own inner depth, she becomes aware there is much to discover, much to receive. And so she learns 'to hearken'. She uses a German word that captures something of the profound awareness that this listening implies: '*hineinhorchen*'. '. . . it seems to me' she writes, 'that this word is untranslatable. Hearkening to myself, to others, to the world.' And in her listening she is searching. 'I listen very intently, with my whole being, and try to fathom the meaning of things.' '*To fathom.*' The word suggests great depths, even a deep darkness of not knowing. 'I keep looking for something,' she writes, 'but don't know what . . .'[27]

One evening two days later, her searching produces one of the most vivid images of this whole early part of the diary, which explodes out of her imagination onto the page. It is an image of depth. She writes: 'There is a really deep well inside me. And in it dwells God. Sometimes I am there, too. But more often stones and grit block the well, and God is buried beneath. Then He must be dug out again.'[28]

Suddenly, without hesitation or embarrassment, she unambiguously names the depth within her from which she senses her life comes. But this life gets blocked, buried, and she is cut off from it. So she defines her task, her mission – to 'dig out' this buried God within her.

## Kneeling down

And then just a few pages further on, another surprise. This time, not an image but a profoundly significant *movement* which seems to take her unawares, and *does* embarrass her:

> This afternoon I suddenly found myself kneeling on the brown coconut matting in the bathroom, my head hidden in my dressing gown, which was slung over the broken cane chair. Kneeling

doesn't really come easily to me, I feel a sort of embarrassment. Why? Probably because of the critical, rational, atheistic bit that is part of me as well. And yet every so often I have a great urge to kneel down with my face in my hands and in this way to find some peace and to listen to that hidden source within me.[29]

In this sudden act, because of the 'critical, rational, atheistic' part of her, she is 'embarrassed'. It is as though one part of her is suddenly gazing in astonishment at what another, deeper part of her is doing. And in her mind she hears the question which the 'atheistic' part of her is loudly asking: What on earth are you doing? What is going on? Her embarrassment is because she is not sure that she knows the answer.

Having done it once, however, the barrier is crossed. Over the months, from September 1941 onwards, as the conditions around her grow uglier, 'kneeling down' becomes part of the pattern of her days as again and again she goes in search of her life. She refers to it more than a dozen times. Gradually it becomes a longing, a necessity even – an expression of what is still a deeply searching spirit.

## The girl who could not kneel but learned to do so . . .

To follow some of the references to this kneeling, in sequence between November 1941 and October 1942, is to trace the path of her search for a deeper life in this God she has discovered, this inner depth she has begun to plumb.

In the autumn of 1941 the search is still intermittent and somewhat romantic. One morning in November she is dreaming about being a writer. She longs 'to give an account' of herself, but where should the focus be, and how to begin? And as she reflects on the moods, the images and the dialogues of her inner life, suddenly she writes: 'And there is God', as though God is another possible way into writing, and she reflects on this act of kneeling down, and how resistant she has been to it – but how profound it is. She gives herself a name, perhaps the title of a future story: 'The girl who could not kneel but learned to do so on the rough coconut matting in an untidy bathroom.' And still there is embarrassment. Not now, though, to do with her mind, but with her body. She has found that this act is very *intimate*. For Etty, this is no cold act of piety: 'Such things', she writes, 'are often more intimate even than sex.'[30]

## A kneeler in training

Slowly this gesture begins to take root. Sometimes it is the prosaic concerns of her role as housekeeper and 'a thousand daily tasks' that drive her to her knees.[31] But as she begins to practise this praying, it gradually becomes no longer a choice but a necessity. She finds it is something she *must* do.

And the sense of necessity seems to come from beyond her. In December she writes: 'Last night . . . I suddenly went down on my knees in the middle of this large room between the steel chairs and the matting. Almost automatically. Forced to the ground by something stronger than myself.' But it is still very new, and still embarrassing, for it brings back echoes of her past, moments of intimacy and tenderness she has known with men. She writes, 'Some time ago I said to myself, "I am a kneeler in training". I was still embarrassed by this act, as intimate as gestures of love that cannot be put into words . . . except by a poet.'[32]

Six days later, she has been reading the tenth chapter of the Gospel of John, and her imagination is caught by images of shepherds and flocks of sheep. The image provides a focus for her praying. As she kneels down 'on the golden matting (a floor covering like a cornfield)', she seeks to gather together 'the wild herds' of her raging feelings, enticing them 'back into the confines of my innermost inner self'. '. . . time after time one must gather oneself together again', she writes, 'around one's very centre. Herding together the disorderly flock of . . . thoughts, emotions, sensations . . . like the good shepherd.'[33]

As she practises this kneeling, she realizes that though it is very new, it really does matter to her. To her surprise, to her embarrassment, she seems to have become genuinely religious.

In the past, I, too, used to be one of those who occasionally exclaimed, 'I *really* am religious, you know.' Or something like that. But now I sometimes actually drop to my knees beside my bed, even on a cold winter night. And I listen in to myself; allow myself to be led, not by anything on the outside, but by what wells up from deep within. It's still no more than a beginning, I know. But it is no longer a shaky beginning, it has already taken root.[34]

Sometimes she kneels down overflowing with a sense of gratitude. In January she writes that she is driven to her knees 'by an unexpected welling up of inner plenitude'.[35] And on 3rd April, 'Good Friday morning', this intensely physical young woman, 'accomplished' in lovemaking, begins to feel that this act of kneeling is what her body has been 'meant and made for':

It is as if my body had been meant and made for the act of kneeling. Sometimes, in moments of deep gratitude, kneeling down becomes an overwhelming urge . . . a gesture embedded in my body, needing to be expressed . . . When I write these things down I still feel a little ashamed, as if I were writing about the most intimate of intimate matters. Much more bashful than if I had to write about my love life. But is there indeed anything as intimate as man's relationship to God?[36]

Increasingly, the kneeling down is a desperate search for protection, so that her fragile humanity – her feeling, hurting soul – may remain alive, and not be poisoned and deadened by the barbarity.

At the end of June 1942 the Nazis bring in a raft of new regulations aimed at isolating and separating off the Jewish population of

Amsterdam. There is a curfew from 8pm to 6am, they cannot stay in the houses of non-Jews, or buy in non-Jewish shops except between 3pm and 5pm, or enter railway stations, or travel on buses or trams, and they can no longer speak to each other because phones are cut off.

This assault on their freedoms casts Etty 'into a hell of alarm and despondency'.[37] As the days pass, there are moments when she particularly feels the exhaustion, the deprivation and the destruction creeping upon them. On 4th July she writes: 'This morning I suddenly had to kneel down on the rough coconut matting in the bathroom, my head bowed so low that it nearly rested on my lap.' As she rests in silence in this posture, her body bent very low, slowly a certain strength begins to return and the arch of her curved back becomes to her like the walls of a cell in which she finds sanctuary and peace. 'I could remain like that for days,' she writes, 'my body like the safe walls of a small cell sheltering me right in its middle.'[38]

## Her body – a sanctuary

So her body becomes her sanctuary, a place of refuge – but also a place of deep sorrow where, amid the terrible cruelty, she holds to her belief in a 'new and kinder day' that will come, which she feels 'growing inside' her: 'They are merciless, totally without pity . . . I suddenly had to kneel down on the hard coconut matting in the bathroom, and the tears poured down my face. And that prayer gave me enough strength for the rest of the day.'[39] This sanctuary will become a movable thing wherever she is sent. On 10th October 1942 she begins her diary that night by wondering whether she can 'bear everything life and these times have in store for me'. She tells herself that when she reaches her limits she will still have her 'folded hands and bended knee. A posture that is not handed down from generation to generation with us Jews. I have had to learn it the hard way.' And she remembers that it was Spier who introduced her to it – her 'most precious inheritance' from him.

It becomes the foundation of her life. In what is almost the final entry of her diary, Etty goes on to define herself and her whole story so far in terms of this gesture. It is that important. The embarrassment is now long since gone, but still a note of wistful surprise is there – as though she can scarcely believe all that has happened to her. 'What a strange story it really is, my story: the girl who could not kneel. Or its variation: the girl who learned to pray. That is my most intimate gesture, more intimate even than being with a man.'[40]

## A great process of growth

So, slowly, hesitantly, at first with embarrassment and then with gratitude, Etty learns to pray. And in the midst of a world 'in the process of collapse', God becomes the ground of her growing confidence – 'I am no longer cut off quite so often from that deep undercurrent within me'; the source of her moral judgements – 'the only certainties about what is right and wrong are those that spring from deep inside'; and the name of the inner 'centre' of her soul. 'God', she prays, '. . . I have assigned an ever larger dwelling place to You . . . The powerful centre spreads its rays to the outermost boundaries.'[41]

And this orientation towards God becomes constant. She writes: 'I now listen all day long to what is within me, and even when I am with others . . . am able to draw strength from the most deeply hidden sources in myself.'[42] And the spatial images that her mind creates in her 'solitary and richly contemplative nights' bear testimony to a profound sense of inner wealth.

> How I love you, my solitary nights! I lie stretched out on my back in my narrow bed, completely abandoned to the night . . . with a sense of how much I am part of a great process of growth. Last night I felt suddenly that my inner landscape was like a vast ripening cornfield . . . inside me are cornfields, growing and ripening.

Of course it was not all bliss on this spiritual journey. There were moments of darkness and doubt. Though her consciousness was being re-fashioned, life for her would never be smooth, unruffled progress. Nor did she think that it should be. For growth to continue she knew the importance of doubt, of *not* knowing, and, though she speaks of her 'inner certainty', she was also suspicious of certainty. In the same entry she writes:

> What a good thing that such states do not persist. One has to be jolted from one's own centre into a state of unrest time and again . . . One must never be too certain of anything, for then all growth comes a halt.[43]

## Mysticism

So the roller-coaster ride went on. But such moments of spiritual awareness were important. They nourished her and took her into a different dimension. Perhaps the most vivid description of such a moment comes, surprisingly, quite early in the diary. She describes how, after 'days of intense inner striving after clarity' – and there was always in her a longing to write – a great peace dawned. She writes as though it happens quite often – a glimpsing of *life* itself which, because of egoism and restlessness, it is so easy to be blind to, and miss.

> . . . I am filled with a sort of bountifulness, even towards myself; . . . And a feeling of being at one with all existence. No longer: I want this or that, but: Life is great and good and fascinating and eternal, and if you dwell so much on yourself and flounder and fluff about, you miss the mighty eternal current that is life. It is in these moments – and I am so grateful for them – that all personal ambition drops away from me, that my thirst for knowledge and understanding comes to rest, and a small piece of eternity descends on me with a sweeping wingbeat.[44]

This is Etty at her most profound. Here we glimpse the inner 'reality' that made her say often that what was going on within her was more real than what was going on outside. This was what sustained her through the hell to come. But this inner life only grew in her because of her courage and honesty, her determination ruthlessly to face up to her own confusions and needs without evasion. 'Mysticism', she wrote, 'must rest on crystal clear honesty, can only come after things have been stripped down to their naked reality.'[45]

## Transformation

Her awakening sense of a profound inner life began to transform her in all kinds of ways.

*Her erotic energy, so all-consuming in her student years, was re-directed.* She knew all too well the destructiveness of desire. Still sometimes it obsessed her. But she also knew its value, when guided, re-focused. 'Yes,' she writes, 'I shall nurture my desire, and perhaps tame it and guide it safely to its destined end.'[46]

*She learnt to absorb and not disown the negative.* In understanding herself she began to find a wise balance, learning to live with her depressive moments and see them in proportion – as muddy ditches in 'a wide blossoming landscape'.[47] As she owned her shadow, it was a preparation for the bearing of a greater darkness.

*The present moment – amid such insecurity – became sacred.* '. . . that cup of coffee', she writes one morning, 'must nowadays be drunk with reverence, for each day it may be our last'.[48] The pressure of the times branded this on her heart. Later, in Westerbork, Matthew 6.34 becomes a mantra to her – she repeats it often: 'Take no thought for the morrow, for the morrow shall take thought for the things of itself. Sufficient unto the day is the evil thereof.'

*Her spiritual imagination continued to nourish her with images of inner space.* Late one night in September 1942 she imagines a whole fleet of sailing ships lying, their treasure undiscovered and lost, at the bottom of an ocean which represents her own inner depths: 'Many treasure fleets have already foundered in my heart,' she writes, 'and I shall try all my life to bring some of the sunken treasure to the surface.'[49]

*Her discipline and watchfulness over herself grew more severe and constant.* In her diary, as she traces the subtle fluctuations of her inner life in her search for what is true, she is tough, 'coming to grips' with herself again and again and insisting: 'Not a single minute of indiscriminate living.'[50]

*The conviction deepened in her that at the root of the human heart lie goodness and love.* Not, despite all the evidence, malice and evil. And so she remains determined that she will refuse hatred.

*And from her spirituality a sense of vocation, even 'destiny' was born in her.* It becomes inevitable that, despite the pleas of many, she will refuse to hide.

And one of the easy-to-miss flowerings of her spirit. *As the world around her grew uglier, her eye and need for beauty grew keener.* One of the loveliest dimensions of Etty's story is her relationship with living things . . . with trees . . . and with flowers, especially flowers.

## The terror

The driving force that took her spirituality deeper was the terror. The terror on the streets, and in the rumours circulating in Amsterdam that Jews across Europe were being rounded up, shipped to concentration camps and exterminated.

As the summer of 1942 approached, life began to deteriorate rapidly. Precious freedoms were taken away. Resources became scarce or unobtainable. Friends disappeared. Surviving in the tasks of daily life became ever more exhausting. The level of anxiety among the Jewish population was rising. Hope and any sense of community became scarce commodities. The world around her was disintegrating. And everywhere there was terrible fear.

## The search for protection

Her need was for protection in this storm. 'The threat grows ever greater,' she writes, 'and terror increases from day to day.' She withdraws into her 'sanctuary'.

> I draw prayer round me like a dark protective wall, withdraw inside it as one might into a convent cell . . . I can imagine times to come when I shall stay on my knees for days on end waiting until the protective walls are strong enough to prevent my going to pieces altogether, my being lost and utterly devastated.[51]

Again and again she goes in search of the secret she has learnt on the rough coconut matting – to withdraw, to be still, and listen.

As she practises this discipline, she finds both protection and, with echoes of the Psalms, a profound comforting from some great source of life which is maternal. She finds that she is both deeply soothed and strangely surprised that among such terrible horrors there could be such profound comfort. One night as she stares out through the open window into the night sky she writes:

> How strange. It is wartime. There are concentration camps. Small barbarity mounts upon small barbarity. I can say of so many of the houses I pass: here the son has been thrown into prison, there the father has been taken hostage, and an eighteen year old boy in that house over there has been sentenced to death. And these streets and houses are all so close to my own. I know how very nervous people are, I know about the mounting human suffering. I know the persecution and oppression and despotism and the impotent fury and the terrible sadism. I know it all . . . And yet – at unguarded moments, when left to myself, I suddenly lie against the naked breast of life, and her arms round me are so gentle and so protective, and my own heartbeat is difficult to describe: so slow and so regular and so

soft, almost muffled, but so constant, as if it would never stop, and so good and merciful as well.

That is also my attitude to life, and I believe that neither war nor any other senseless human atrocity will ever be able to change it.[52]

In the midst of war this young woman does not go to pieces. She is held. And as her faith grows stronger, a deeper insight into the mystery of this life with God is born in her.

## God cannot help

She comes to realize that the God who in the Psalms is 'protective' and 'good and merciful' *cannot help them*. But she also knows more deeply than she knows anything that she cannot live without this God, without 'kneeling down' – constantly. She has learnt again and again in the midst of the fear, that to 'kneel down' is to re-discover her life. It is to reach into the wide, open plains of the inner land-scape of her spacious heart and be renewed at the depths of her being. And yet it dawns upon her as she struggles to comprehend the extent of the suffering that the God before whom she kneels *cannot help them*. She has seen too much pain and misery to believe anymore that he can. She has watched too many vulnerable mothers in despair, witnessed too many men being humiliated and broken, heard too many desperate cries for help, seen too many people rounded up and imprisoned, and heard too many stories of what is happening to her fellow Jews in concentration camps . . . *to believe any more that God can help.*

As one reads her, one is reminded of the words of Dietrich Bon-hoeffer writing to his friend Eberhard Bethge from his prison cell in Flossenberg just nine months before he was hanged by the Nazis. Bonhoeffer wrote of the God who is 'weak and powerless in the world'. 'Before God and with him', he wrote, 'we live without God.' 'God allows himself to be edged out of the world and on to the cross' and so is 'weak and powerless'. But Bonhoeffer insists that 'that is exactly the way, the only way, in which he can be with us and help us'.[53]

Etty arrives at the same insight – but as a woman. As she contemplates the helplessness of her people, their suffering and their fate, her task, she realizes, is not in bitterness to abandon faith in this God, but *to look after him and care for him*, for she knows that if they lose God they lose everything – their humanity, their integrity, their beauty as people, their life. They will disintegrate. 'What matters', she writes later, 'is not whether we preserve our lives at any cost, but *how* we preserve them.'[54] And so, God becomes to her *a vulnerable Presence*, to be looked after and cherished in the human heart.


## 'We must defend your dwelling place inside us to the last'

Early one Sunday morning she prays:

> Dear God, these are anxious times. Tonight . . . I lay in the dark with burning eyes as scene after scene of human suffering passed before me. . . . I shall try to help You, God, to stop my strength ebbing away, though I cannot vouch for it in advance. But one thing is becoming increasingly clear to me: that You cannot help us, that we must help You to help ourselves. And that is all we can manage these days and also all that really matters: that we safeguard that little piece of You, God, in ourselves . . . Alas, there doesn't seem to be much You Yourself can do about our circumstances, about our lives. Neither do I hold You responsible. You cannot help us, but we must help You and defend Your dwelling place inside us to the last. There are, it is true, some who, even at this late stage, are putting their vacuum cleaners and silver forks and spoons in safekeeping instead of guarding You, dear God. And there are those who want to put their bodies in safekeeping but who are nothing more now than a shelter for a thousand fears and bitter feelings. And they say,

'I shan't let them get me into their clutches.' But they forget that no one is in their clutches who is in Your arms.[55]

And from this insight – that the God who cannot help them must be helped and cared for – come some of the most tender and moving passages of the diary as she shares the gentle conversations she has with this God whom she must look after.

> The jasmine behind my house has been completely ruined by the rains and storms of the last few days; its white blossoms are floating about in muddy black pools on the low garage roof. But somewhere inside me the jasmine continues to blossom undisturbed, just as profusely and delicately as ever it did. And it spreads its scent round the House in which you dwell, O God. You can see, I look after You, I bring You not only my tears and my foreboding on this stormy, grey Sunday morning, I even bring you scented jasmine. And I shall bring You all the flowers I shall meet on my way, and truly there are many of those. I shall try to make You at home always. Even if I should be locked up in a narrow cell and a cloud should drift past my small barred window, then I shall bring you that cloud, oh God, while there is still the strength in me to do so. I cannot promise You anything for tomorrow, but my intentions are good, You can see.[56]

## Lover and beloved

They are the words of a lover, offering flowers, scented jasmine, to her beloved. And there is vulnerability and need in both.

And so, out of the crucible of the Holocaust emerged a profound theology of vulnerable Presence which led this extraordinary young woman to triumph over the evil that threatened to engulf her.

But what she achieved was not based on sentiment. Her triumph was the fruit of a remarkable discipline developed over a very short space of time as she battled against the power of the menace all around them which overshadowed everything. She knew that, if she gave in to it, it would weaken and destroy her. And so, as the clamour of the fear rises, she cultivates an inner solitude; as the contagion of the fear spreads, she practises an inner detachment; as the cancer of the fear eats away the spirit of those around her, she is rigorously watchful against it in her own mind; as the cries of the fear become an awful cacophony, she learns to listen deeply to the silence of her own heart; as she faces up to and accepts what the fear points to – their inevitable end – she consciously nourishes a profound inner freedom. And at the heart of this rigorously disciplined inner life was her openness to the Mystery of the Divine experienced within her as vulnerable Presence.

It was this that fortified her refusal to hate.

Two of the diary exercise books
*Patrick Woodhouse*

# Chapter 3

---

# Refusing to Hate

*And then I knew: I should take the field against hatred.*

Beginning in the early 1930s, Jews all across Europe became victims of a terrible and ancient hatred. Anti-semitism did not of course begin in Hitler's Germany. There is a long and ugly history that can be traced back to the very beginnings of Christianity. Christian civilization has been marred by a succession of persecutions and pogroms, of which Etty's mother was another victim, fleeing from Russia to the Netherlands in 1907. However, in post-First World War Germany, at the time of the great depression, this hatred developed with a ferocity hitherto unknown. Blaming the Jews for Germany's ills was at the heart of Nazi propaganda as Hitler rose to power, and ridding Germany of the Jews so that the nation would be racially 'pure' became a central policy of the Third Reich. It was to develop ultimately into the 'Final Solution', the attempted extermination of an entire people.

As Hitler's armies advanced across Europe into other nations, and the Jews of those nations became targets together with those Jews who had fled Nazi Germany during the 1930s, it was entirely natural that among these persecuted Jewish populations there developed a reciprocal hatred of the Germans. This was true in Amsterdam during the early 1940s as its large Jewish population began to suffer the effects of a whole series of measures against them.

It is against this background that in March 1941 Etty began her diary. One of the noticeable things about the diary is that, in the early part, details of the war itself crop up comparatively infrequently. It is as though she is too caught up with the narrative of her feelings and friendships, her ideas and reading – and above all the complex story of her therapy and the all-consuming relationship with Julius Spier – to allow it to intrude.

## 'The problem of our age'

Within a few pages of the beginning of the diary, however, she does write about hatred. It cannot be avoided.

> It is the problem of our age: hatred against the Germans poisons everyone's mind. 'Let the bastards drown, the lot of them' – such sentiments have become part and parcel of our daily speech and sometimes make one feel that life these days has grown impossible.[1]

A few lines further on she adds: '. . . indiscriminate hatred is the worst thing there is. It is a sickness of the soul.' And she insists: 'Hatred does not lie in my nature.'

Later, in a September entry she indicates just how ingrained hatred had become in the mind of the Jewish population when she recounts a conversation with a student acquaintance:

> . . . she thinks that all eighty million Germans must be exterminated. Not a single one must be kept alive. This because I said that I could not live with the kind of hatred so many people nowadays force upon themselves against their better nature. And then it all came bursting out. How ugly, how degrading, how horrible!

Etty is so stirred up by this conversation that although she goes home intending to do some writing, she can't contain herself and bursts into the room where her student friend Bernard is having a conversation with one of his friends. She asks them directly: 'Tell me, do you also think that every last German ought to be exterminated?' Their immediate response is unequivocal, 'Yes, of course', as though it were absurd to think anything else. She adds, 'a passionate and furious discussion ensued'.[2]

However, though she is appalled, she does not entirely escape the contagion. Sometimes she too cannot help herself. 'Sometimes when I read the papers or hear reports of what is happening all around, I am suddenly beside myself with anger, cursing and swearing at the Germans.' And she owns up to a particular focus for this hatred – her close friend in the house, Käthe the cook, whom she is very fond of ('like a second mother to me') but who is German. 'I know I do it deliberately to hurt Käthe, to work off my anger as best I can . . . sometimes I cannot bear the thought that she cannot share my hatred . . .' A few lines further on she continues:

> The whole nation must be destroyed root and branch. And now
> and then I say nastily, 'They're all scum', and at the same time
> I feel terribly ashamed and deeply unhappy but can't stop, even
> though I know that it's all wrong.[3]

## 'I cannot hate'

Perhaps the simple act of writing this down – and she has been keeping her diary for less than a week – has an effect on Etty, for it is the first and last time that she succumbs to this 'sickness of the soul'. She reflects at length on it all and then concludes:

> To sum up, this is what I really want to say: Nazi barbarism
> evokes the same kind of barbarism in ourselves . . . We have to
> reject that barbarism within us, we must not fan the hatred
> within us, because if we do, the world will not be able to pull
> itself one inch further out of the mire.[4]

So right at the beginning of the diary she takes a stand against hatred. She will not indulge in it. In this respect, within the circle of her friends, her life is a deep contradiction. One might suspect that this declaration arose merely in a moment of youthful idealism on the part of a naive young woman who had not yet faced the full horror and brutality of an enemy who was bent on their destruction and regarded Jews as less than human. However, as her story unfolds and she shares her people's increasingly desperate plight, her conviction deepens and is expressed in even more resolute language. While at the beginning she merely says 'hatred does not lie in my nature', and 'we have to reject that barbarism within us', later she goes further, saying hatred is something which for her is simply impossible. '*I cannot hate.*' It is no longer just that she thinks it wrong and degrading. If she is to remain true to herself, *it cannot be part of her nature*.

This deeper conviction dawns on her after a particular incident one morning when Jews have been gathered together in a hall in order to be registered. During this process she is shouted at and threatened by an aggressive young Gestapo officer. After describing the incident she writes: 'Something else about this morning: the perception, very strongly borne in, that despite all the suffering and injustice, I cannot hate others.'[5] It is a conviction which she holds to right up to the end when she is put on the train to Auschwitz.

'I cannot hate others.' What does she mean? And in the light of what the Jews in Amsterdam and Holland faced through these months and years, we may well ask how was it possible to hold to this? What understandings and disciplines of the mind enabled her to sustain this ideal?

## Truth

Her sense that hatred was, for her at least, simply not possible, grew from her commitment to truth. With rare passion, Etty was concerned with what is true. This makes her frustrated and upset in the 'acrimonious discussions' which go on among the small international community of her household when they start talking about hatred of the Germans. She finds their discussions superficial and sterile.

> . . . these discussions are hardly ever concerned with real politics, with any attempt to grasp major political trends or to fathom the underlying currents. On the contrary, everything looks so clear-cut and ugly, which is why it is so unpleasant to discuss politics in the present climate . . .[6]

What frustrates her and makes her so dislike these discussions is because there is no serious attempt to search out what is *true*, no intellectual effort to try to clarify 'the major trends' in their history that have led to this war. A discussion on the history and myths of the German people, or their social, psychological and economic needs since their defeat, or the effects of the Treaty of Versailles, or how the Nazis had come to power and what the Jews represented to them – this would have been useful. But her housemates are not interested in such questions. Everything is just 'clear-cut', 'ugly' – and full of hatred.

The search for truth was a driving force in Etty's makeup. It was the intensity of her determination to discover her own personal truth that drove her on in her work with Spier, determined to comprehend the complexity of herself. Later she came to understand her vocation as the seeing and bearing witness to what was more deeply true in the terrible times in which she lived. And she knew that truth is indivisible. If it is complex and multidimensional in the personal lives of individuals, it is also complex and multidimensional in the political affairs of nations. And this is why she cannot be doing with hatred, for to hate short-circuits the whole demanding and complex process of understanding – of fathoming underlying currents – in both people and nations. It closes down people's minds, diverts precious energy into resentment, stops the asking of difficult questions, and produces superficial and easy answers. Then discovering what is true becomes impossible.

And when the search for truth is abandoned, a terrible blindness overcomes people. She would have seen and heard it for herself in the rise of Nazism in Germany through the 1930s – a whole nation falling prey to lies and propaganda – clear-cut, very ugly and full of hatred.

## 'The small naked human being amid the monstrous wreckage'

But there was a second reason why she could not hate. As her story continued, both in Amsterdam and then in Westerbork, she remained determined to see the faces of human beings beneath the ugly masks of war. She refused to concede that the hatreds and enmities of war are the final story. There is a deeper script about human beings in all their vulnerability belonging together across the divides; and signs of this deeper connectedness can be glimpsed in people's faces, in the tell-tale signs of their humanity. It must be held to, even across the chasms that war creates.

Her search for this common humanity is revealed in the same incident of registration in which she is shouted at by the young Gestapo officer. As she stands waiting with all the others, she watches this young man pacing up and down, 'making no attempt to hide his irritation', and 'looking for pretexts to shout at the helpless Jews'. When it is her turn to stand before his desk, he starts to bawl at her because of the expression on her face. She is smiling, but he thinks she is 'smirking'. She says, 'I didn't mean to, it is my usual expression.' 'Don't give me that,' he yells, 'get the hell out of here', his face saying 'I'll deal with you later.' '. . . that', she says, 'was presumably meant to scare me to death, but the device was too transparent. I am not easily frightened. Not because I am brave, but because I know that I am dealing with human beings . . .'

Behind the transparent mask of this soldier Etty sees a 'pitiful' young man – 'harassed and driven, sullen and weak' – pitiful in his need to bully and humiliate. 'I should have liked to start treating him there and then,' she writes, 'for I know that pitiful young men like that are dangerous as soon as they are let loose on mankind.'[7]

This conviction, that behind the ugly realities of war there are fallible and damaged human beings, becomes so fundamental to her that it eventually transforms how she sees everything – even a world as dark as Westerbork. 'I try to look things straight in the eye,' she writes, 'even the worst crimes, to discover the small, naked human being amid the monstrous wreckage caused by man's senseless deeds.'[8] And for Etty, the first 'small, naked human being' that must be seen, listened to and cared for, is ourselves.

## Ideological thinking

This truth came to colour her whole understanding of life, particularly when she was in touch with friends whom she believed were easily prey to hatred because they were trapped in ideological thinking – and so had become blind to the personal dimension.

Europe in the 1930s was riven by debate and violent conflict over different ideologies – socialism, communism and fascism. As a student at Amsterdam, Etty was a member of the 'Students' League against War and Fascism', and many of her closest friends were committed socialists and communists. She would have taken part in many political discussions and seen passionately held beliefs harden into ideological conviction. She would have seen hatred growing, and, with the attempt to force it into pre-set moulds, truth becoming a casualty.

By 1941 her student years were largely behind her but she had become deeply suspicious of all ideological thinking – either political or indeed religious. 'An element of deception necessarily steals into every "ism" . . .'[9] she says, and, referring to the political creed with which she was most comfortable, she writes: 'Socialism lets in hatred against everything that is not socialist through the back door . . .'[10] At this time she was very drawn to the writings of Jung, and his thinking would have affirmed her own growing understandings. Jung regarded 'isms' as 'the viruses of our day, and responsible for greater disasters than any mediaeval plague . . .'[11]

Her suspicion extended to all fixed systems of thought.

> We form fixed ideas . . . in order to have some certainty in this
> confusing, ever shifting life of ours, but in doing so we sacrifice
> real life with all its nuances and elements of surprise, as well as
> selling it short.
>    Life cannot be forced into a system . . . And it is to systems
> sometimes built with great hardship that men sacrifice reality
> and truth.[12]

And this applied to religious as well as political systems. They too
cause division and hatred.

In November 1941 she is listening to a religious discussion between Spier and Werner Levie, a Zionist friend, about 'Christ and the
Jews'. Both men become passionate in their views. As the debate ends,
Etty comments: 'Two philosophies, sharply defined, brilliantly pre-
sented, rounded off; defended with passion and vigour. But I can't
help feeling that every hotly championed philosophy hides a little lie.
That it must fall short of "the truth"'.[13]

In her mind, any 'hotly championed philosophy' is cause for suspicion. People embrace them with fervour, but the very fact that they
are 'hotly championed' gives the game away. They are a deception.
Life cannot be packaged up and fenced in like that. Such 'rounded
off' systems of thought divide and kindle hatred – and, most important for her, ideological fervour is a distraction from the fundamental task of all seekers of truth which is to explore what lies in the
complex and needy hearts of human beings – our own first.

In developing her passionate belief that hatred needs to be addressed
in the context of persons, she acknowledges the wider dimension – that
the politics of whole societies can become evil, and that

> systems grow too big for men, and hold them in a satanic grip,
> the builders no less than the victims of the system, much as
> large edifices and spires, created by men's hands, tower high

above us, dominate us, yet may collapse over our heads and bury us.[14]

But the debates about politics and ideology that surround this war fail to engage or interest her. She feels that she has been through it all before in 'the post-war literature' of the First World War. 'So much rebelliousness, so much hatred, the passion, the arguments, the call for social justice, the class struggle etc., we have been through it all.'[15] In her mind it does not get to the root of things. Only attention to the human heart, she believes, will root out hatred, not the tired politics of her time.

## A humanist vision

This humanist vision comes over most clearly in a part of her diary where she addresses directly her old friend and former lover, Klaas Smelik, who was a convinced ideologue. Smelik, whom she had first met in Deventer in 1934 when she was just 19 years old, and with whom she had had a six-month affair, was a Trotskyite. He was a committed anti-fascist and member of the Dutch Communist Party and then later the Revolutionary–Socialist Labour Party, organizations that believed in ideological struggle and class conflict.

The diary entry, dated 23rd September 1942, refers back to her time at Westerbork in the summer of that year. She describes one of her colleagues in the Jewish Council, to whom the Germans had given authority in running the camp, who was imperious and cruel in the way he treated his fellow Jews. She begins by directly referring to the issue of hatred – the hatred of the class war – and the need to go beyond hatred, and see people.

We shan't get anywhere with hatred Klaas. Appearances are so often deceptive. Take one of my colleagues. I see him often in my thoughts. The most striking thing about him is his inflexible, rigid neck. He hates our persecutors with an undying hatred, presumably with good reason. But he himself is a bully.

He would make a model concentration camp guard. I often watched him standing beside the camp entrance to admit his hunted fellow Jews, never a pleasant sight . . . When I saw him walking about among the others with his rigid neck and imperious look and his ever-present short pipe, I always thought, all he needs is a whip in his hand, it would suit him to perfection.

But still I never hated him. I found him much too fascinating for that. Now and then I really felt terribly sorry for him. He had such an unhappy, miserable mouth, if the truth be told.

She goes on to reveal more about what lies below the surface in this man, which his outward appearance belies. She tells of how alone he was. 'There was never any real contact between him and others, and he would give such covert, hungry looks whenever other people were friendly to each other.' She tells how he had tried to commit suicide several times, and had spent time in a mental institution, and in the end he hanged himself. She adds: 'I felt such deep deep pity for him.' She sees that all his bullying behaviour grew out of a deep unattended-to need, a profound loneliness of the spirit. This is where the roots of tyranny lie.

But she also knows that you cannot cast the mote out of someone else's eye until you have dealt with the beam in your own. The letter continues:

Klaas, all I really wanted to say is this: we have so much work to do on ourselves that we shouldn't even be thinking of hating our so-called enemies. We are hurtful enough to one another as it is. And I don't really know what I mean when I say there are bullies and bad characters among our own people, for no one is really 'bad' deep down.

I should have liked to reach out to that man with all his fears, I should have liked to trace the source of his panic, to drive him ever deeper into himself; that is the only thing we can do, Klaas, in times like these . . .

I repeat with the same old passion, although I am gradually beginning to think that I am being tiresome, 'it is the only thing we can do, Klaas, I see no alternative: each of us must turn inward and destroy in himself all that he thinks he ought to destroy in others. And remember that every atom of hate we add to this world makes it still more inhospitable.'

And you, Klaas, dogged old class fighter that you have always been, dismayed and astonished at the same time, say, 'But that – that is nothing but Christianity!'

And I, amused by your confusion, retort quite coolly, 'Yes, Christianity, and why ever not?'[16]

At the heart of this creed, expressed with warmth and affection to her old friend, is her acute perceptiveness, her capacity to *see* people. She does not miss the smallest detail – the rigid neck, the short pipe, the unhappy mouth, the covert hungry look – but she sees with compassion. So how can she hate? But she knows Klaas of old, knows that he will not listen.

However, sometimes, in her eagerness to explore her thinking, her old political friends *do* listen to her. She tells of how on a freezing cold day in February 1942 she is waiting at a tram stop with a student friend, Jan Bool. The question of hatred comes up again. They have been discussing how some professors and teachers they have known have been taken prisoner and are being demoralized and humiliated by the Germans. Suddenly Jan asks: 'What is it in human beings that makes them want to destroy others?' Etty replies: 'Human beings, you say, but remember that you're one yourself.' And she continues, '. . . strangely enough he seemed to acquiesce, grumpy, gruff old Jan.' Her surprise is no doubt because she knows him well too – he is politically involved in the anti-fascist movement, is active in the students' resistance, and is a member of the Dutch Communist Party. Perhaps she expects some kind of political or ideological lecture, not silence and apparent agreement. Etty does not quite trust his acquiescence and becomes quite preachy.

'The rottenness of others is in us, too', I continued to preach at him. 'I see no other solution, I really see no other solution than to turn inward and to root out all the rottenness there. I no longer believe that we can change anything in the world until we have first changed ourselves. And that seems to me the only lesson to be learned from this war. That we must look into ourselves and nowhere else.'

Her little homily ends, and to her evident surprise, Jan agrees.

[He] . . . so unexpectedly agreed with everything I said, was approachable and interested and no longer proffered any of his hard-boiled social theories. Instead, he said, 'Yes it's too easy to turn your hatred loose on the outside, to live for nothing but the moment of revenge. We must try to do without that.' We stood there in the cold waiting for the tram, Jan with his great purple chilblained hands and his toothache. Our professors are in prison, another of Jan's friends has been killed, and there are so many other sorrows, but all we said to each other was, 'It is too easy to feel vindictive.'
   That really was the bright spot of today.[17]

'It is too easy to feel vindictive.' As she moves away from the aridity of so much ideological discussion on to this more personal ground she has, to her surprise, found a companion: grumpy, gruff old Jan – with his 'hard-boiled social theories'.

## Hatred – and fear

Etty's commitment to truth, her commitment to a common humanity deeper than the divides of war, her suspicion of ideologies – all these were reasons why she resisted hatred.
   But there was a deeper reason, and that was fear. She knew that if she began to hate she would begin to fear, that fear and hatred are

two poisons of the spirit which feed off each other. Fear generates hatred and hatred maximizes fear, and fear weakens the spirit and in the end destroys people. Every day she saw around her the effects that fear was having in the lives of the Jewish community.

Perhaps if Etty feared anything, it was fear itself. Like a terrible contagion spreading through the population, she saw people becoming desperate through fear as the threat grew of being rounded up and taken away. She saw them becoming frantic in their search for a place in which to hide – frantic to get out of the clutches of this barbarism. And in their fear, their humanity was steadily destroyed until they were 'no more than a shelter for a thousand fears and bitter feelings'. Or worse, in the camp she saw how fear could drive people to the borders of insanity so that they no longer wished to feel at all. What fear was doing to those around her filled her with compassion and a desire to remain alive as a thinking, feeling person herself, in the middle of it all, for their sakes.

> At night as I lay in the camp on my plank bed surrounded by women and girls, gently snoring, dreaming aloud, quietly sobbing, tossing and turning, women and girls who often told me during the day, 'We don't want to think, we don't want to feel, otherwise we are sure to go out of our minds', I was sometimes filled with an infinite tenderness, and lay awake for hours . . . and I prayed, 'Let me be the thinking heart of these barracks.'[18]

## A lack of inner preparation

Refusing to hate was one way of coping with the threat of fear, but was it enough? She realized that the mind needs inner defences to be prepared; that buttresses and bulwarks of the spirit need to be put in place if these deadly contagions are to be prevented from infiltrating the mind with their terrible power to destroy people's humanity.

One place where fear and hate seemed to be at permanent fever pitch was the Jewish Council which was set up by the Nazis to deal with all the questions and issues of the Jewish community. As the persecution intensified, its office was at the eye of the storm of fear. In July 1942, Etty began to work there as a secretary. She disliked it intensely, yet she cared about those who worked alongside her in their confusion and terror. In her diary she wrote about their fear, 'the deadly fear I saw in all those faces . . . All those faces, my God, those faces! I hope to be a centre of peace in that madhouse.'[19] On the previous evening she had written: 'The greatest cause of suffering in so many of our people is their utter lack of inner preparation.'[20] She saw that over the time since the occupation began, so many of her fellow Jews had built up no defences against what was now coming upon them. By contrast, she had been preparing inwardly for months. She had faced up to her fear; she had learnt to steady herself and find a deep still centre; she had struggled against the temptation to indulge in illusion; and as we shall see, as the situation deteriorated she became engaged in a constant mental rehearsal for what she saw was inevitable. By anticipating it, she would rob it of its power.

Yet paradoxically, as well as anticipating she also focused on other 'realities'. This too was part of her 'inner preparation', perhaps a more crucial part. Over the months of late 1941 and early 1942 she consciously turned her gaze elsewhere.

## 'My "realities" may be different . . .'

We have already noted how, in the earlier part of the diary, the war intrudes only rarely. Initially this may simply have been because her personal needs were so pressing that she had little mental space for anything else. But as the personal turmoils of the first half of 1941 slowly recede, and the diary moves on into the first half of 1942, there is a deliberate distancing from the agonies of war and persecution, a refusal to become mentally over-involved before she has to.

She immerses herself in other 'realities' that she finds so much richer. At times the war seems almost absent, such is her determination to continue her life and garner her inner resources. Her involvement in these other things means that she is not so exposed to fear. But occasionally she wonders if she is being irresponsible because she is 'not in touch with reality'. But immediately she has questioned herself over this, she is clear about her response: 'I don't think so . . . To me the greatest reality is still the sun on the hyacinths, the rabbit, the chocolate pudding, Beethoven, the grey hair at his temple . . .'[21] However, the questioning did not go away. In a letter of 1943 she wrote: 'Why don't I keep my feet on the ground? Am I a dreamer? Oh please let me be, there have to be people like me too. My realities may be different from what most people call reality, but still they *are* realities.'[22]

And what, over the months of the spring of 1942, were her 'realities'? Her emotional security with her men – she came home to Han Wegerif and simultaneously fell more and more in love with Spier; her rich intellectual diet – Jung, Dostoyevsky, other Russian writers, and Rilke, more and more Rilke; her contacts and friendships in the household and with those who came for lessons in Russian; her spiritual reading – her relationship with St Matthew, her delight in St Augustine, her daily immersion in the Psalms; and when the war does intrude and she feels overwhelmed, her kneeling down – 'the only adequate gesture left to us in these times'.[23] At the heart of it all there was her beloved desk, scattered with books and always with a flower beside her. It was her secret oasis, 'my true hub',[24] a small island of serenity and calm where late at night and in the early hours of the morning she wrote, wrote for hours, pausing just now and then to gaze out of her window across to the Rijksmuseum, or at night up into the vastness of the night sky, or simply to observe her two trees outside her window, climbing into the sky 'like two vertical pathways, two signposts in a dark landscape'.[25]

The writing of the diary itself was what perhaps most profoundly nourished her. As she relates her daily activities, ponders her feelings, reflects on her encounters, copies out her favourite passages, muses over her moods, and traces with her gift for words the inner contours of her intensely alive spirit, she inhabits a world infinitely richer and more nourishing than the barbarity outside.

And like a bright thread woven through the varied pattern of her days, she writes again and again of her love of flowers. As the ugliness of war threatened to distort the perception of everything, her constant delight in the beauty of flowers only intensified. There are constant references. She bids good night and good morning to the small yellow and purple crocuses in the chocolate tin beside her bed; she watches her red and white tulip buds bending gracefully towards one another; she delights in 'the sprays of flowering cherry from the little woman with whom I'm reading Jung . . . standing . . . in blossom, vernal and tender pink against the pale grey curtain';[26] she notices how her small narcissi light up a portrait on the wall above her 'like radiant stars';[27] she feels 'the almost unbearable beauty of the rose-red sweet peas standing there amidst my books';[28] she muses about a small red, faded anemone pressed between the pages of a book; she wonders at the colour of an open yellow tea rose – it 'makes one believe in God';[29] and she is enchanted by her 'Japanese lilies with their wide-open orange-red cups' standing 'as outlandish and bizarre as mysterious fairly-tale dragons'.[30] Sometimes her wonder and astonishment at the beauty of flowers eclipse everything else in the day:

> . . . today's real experience was the magnolia in the corner of Tide's room, whose mysterious beauty almost scared me stiff. I stood open-mouthed for nearly five minutes as if nailed to the floor . . . I couldn't believe there could be so much beauty, couldn't take it all in. I could hardly tear myself away from the flowers, stroked the leaves very gently with the tips of my fingers and almost asked Tide, 'Please may I pay a visit to your magnolia every day?'[31]

In the western Protestant Church at least, beauty is a neglected aspect in theological study, but it is crucial. 'Late have I loved you, beauty so old and new' wrote St Augustine, directly addressing God in terms of 'beauty'.[32] An eye for beauty played a key part in the survival of Etty's humanity. It helped her to go on seeing clearly when so many others were blinded with pettiness and hatred.

And her delight in flowers was an outward reflection of what went on flowering in her heart. As so much in her world was stripped away or smashed to fragments, the flowers she delights in reflect back to her the stubborn enduring beauty of her inner life. Whatever was happening around her, still she could give flowers to others and receive flowers from others and she could buy flowers for herself. Right to the end of her time in Amsterdam, even when all forms of transport were denied her, she would go out of her way to buy flowers. They were one of her deepest 'realities':

> Last night, walking that long way home through the rain with the blister on my foot, I still made a short detour to seek out a flower stall, and went home with a large bunch of roses. And there they are. They are just as real as all the misery I witness each day.[33]

## Life's immutable generosity

The early months of 1942 were a time, extraordinarily, of great richness. There are moments when she is overwhelmed with gratitude – can hardly believe her life.

> It's happened to me a few times recently – in the street or wherever I chance to be, I stop with bated breath for a moment and have to ask myself, is this really *my* life? So full, so rich, so intense and so beautiful?[34]

Part of this richness was her awareness of what she has been through in dealing with her past which she now holds, 'assimilated', within her, '. . . everything I have ever experienced . . . lies at rest deep within me, assimilated and in good shape, and that is perhaps why I feel so satisfied, so rich, so replete, so filled with experience.'[35]

She does not forget those who are suffering, but 'life's immutable generosity'[36] wells up within her, and she is conscious of the inner capital that she is accumulating.

> This afternoon, during the Beethoven, I suddenly had to bow my head and pray for all who are lingering in freezing concentration camps, prayed God to give them strength to remember the good moments of their lives, just as in hard times I shall remember this day and many days during the last year, and draw what strength I need from them lest I become embittered with life. We must see to it that we daily grow in strength to bear the times that will come.[37]

Her 'realities', her inner resources, her deliberate distancing from the war – all these play their part in saving her from any bitterness, in preparing her for what is to come. Through these months there is a consistent vein of confidence in her writing. In late April, sitting at her 'trusty desk, surrounded by books, chestnut twigs, and celandine plus the pencil sketch of S's head diagonally across from me on the wall', she writes, 'I honestly feel I can cope with these frightful days, that I'll get through them . . . I think I have grown mature enough now to bear a great many hard things in life and yet not to grow too hard inside.'[38]

And in July, when the level of threat against her is very great, she again reaffirms what lies, even more strongly, in her 'deepest and best' self: '*it is not in my nature to tilt against the savage cold-blooded fanatics who clamour for our destruction. I am not afraid of them either*'[39] (my italics).

But if you refuse to hate, there is a consequence that follows. Etty realized that hatred is a way of avoiding pain, a kind of weapon that people use to defend themselves against their own suffering. She writes of her colleagues in the Jewish Council: 'They don't even suffer deep down. They just hate . . .'[40]

If you will not hate, what must follow?

## 'You must be able to bear your sorrow'

From early on in her diary, Etty is clear that the only truly creative response to suffering is to bear it. She writes:

> . . . you must be able to bear your sorrow; even if it seems to crush you, you will be able to stand up again, for human beings are so strong, and your sorrow must become an integral part of yourself . . . you mustn't run away from it, but bear it like an adult. Do not relieve your feelings through hatred, do not seek to be avenged on all German mothers, for they too, sorrow for their slain and murdered sons. Give your sorrow all the space and shelter in yourself that is its due, for if everyone bears his grief honestly and courageously, the sorrow that now fills the world will abate. But if you do not clear a decent shelter for your sorrow, and instead reserve most of the space inside you for hatred and thoughts of revenge – from which new sorrows will be born for others – then sorrow will never cease in this world and will multiply.[41]

'Give your sorrow all the space and shelter in yourself that is its due' . . . clear 'a decent shelter' for it. It is an extraordinary image. She sees that the sorrow which people face is immense, but somehow it must be accommodated, somehow it must be given sufficient space in the heart. There is no alternative. If it is not owned and embraced, but disregarded and left to fester inside a person buried and unacknowledged, then it will wreak havoc. It will either destroy the person, or become a distorting demonic power in the personality fuelling bitterness and hatred.

## A universal person

Sorrow is also, she says, not a private fenced-in thing. It crosses boundaries. As you learn to sorrow, you will find yourself united with all sorrowing peoples, even the sorrowing hearts of the enemy, even with German mothers, 'for they too sorrow for their slain and murdered sons'. And not just mothers, as though it is the men who fight and the women who wait at home and weep, for elsewhere she writes, '. . . German soldiers suffer as well. There are no frontiers between suffering people . . .'[42]

So Etty becomes a universal person, and her reflection on suffering is an extension of her idea that war is, in the end, human-sized. Human in its origins, in the failure to love; and human in its terrible consequences, in its griefs and sorrows.

She believes too, that if we make sufficient space in our lives for them, sorrow and suffering can be redemptive.

In the first of two long letters from the camp about the conditions there, which were published illegally during the war – and these contain her greatest writing – she says:

> . . . if we abandon the hard facts that we are forced to face, if we give them no shelter in our heads and hearts, do not allow them to settle and change into impulses through which we can grow and from which we can draw meaning – then we are not a viable generation.
>
> It is not easy – and no doubt less easy for us Jews than for anyone else – yet if we have nothing to offer a desolate postwar world but bodies saved at any cost, if we fail to draw new meaning from the deep wells of our distress and despair, then it will not be enough.[43]

Her own story of transformation from chaos to selfhood is testimony to the fact that such redemption in a human life can occur. And surely that is precisely where her understanding of personal redemption – through bearing what has to be borne – comes from.

In the weeks and months of her work with Spier, she had learnt very personally to bear her own pain and alienation as a child and as a young person. And it had set her free. The lesson had gone deep.

From early on in the diary she refers often to this need 'to bear sorrow'. And she finds this lesson echoed in the writings of others. On 15th December 1941 she quotes from a book by Suares on Dostoyevsky: '. . . we must be acquainted with pain. Real man is neither master of his pain, nor fugitive from it, nor its slave, he must be pain's redeemer.' And on the same day from Walter Rathenau in his *Letters to a Woman in Love:* 'We are here to take some of the world's suffering upon ourselves by bearing our breast to it, not to increase it by our own violence.'[44]

But her greatest teacher was Spier himself. On the previous page in the diary she had written: 'Paradoxical though it may sound: S. heals people by teaching them to suffer and accept.'[45]

It was of course Spier who encouraged her to read the New Testament; it was he who encouraged her to reflect on the figure of Christ; and it was Spier – a Jew – whom she remembers once telling her that he dreamt that 'Christ himself came to baptize me.'[46] In this question of hatred, of bearing suffering and finding redemption, Spier's attraction to the person of Christ may have been a deep influence upon her. We may wonder whether, as she wrote about sorrow, she pondered the Man of Sorrows who was 'acquainted with grief' and who in the Gospel of Matthew, which she so loved, said, 'blessed are the sorrowful'.

It is striking that in a kind of final flourish against hatred, she ends the first of her two long letters about the camp at Westerbork by referring to the writings of 'the Jew Paul' in the New Testament:

> I know that those who hate have good reason to do so. But why should we always have to choose the cheapest and easiest way? It has been brought home forcibly to me here how every atom of hatred added to the world makes it an even more inhospitable place. And I also believe, childishly perhaps but stubbornly, that the earth will become more habitable again only through the love that the Jew Paul described to the citizens of Corinth in the thirteenth chapter of his first letter.[47]

Etty c. 1942
*Collection Jewish Historical Museum, Amsterdam*

# Chapter 4

# Losing Her Life

*I have already died a thousand deaths in a thousand concentration camps.*

Before exploring the next stage of Etty Hillesum's journey, which took her from her world in Amsterdam into Westerbork, let us reflect on the story so far.

In the first chapter we looked at her childhood and family and reflected particularly on the earlier part of the diary. It was a time of healing and integration. Out of her chaos, order began to emerge. She came to understand and like herself. Her wild, erotic nature began to be transformed and directed towards something infinitely greater.

The second chapter traced the growth of an unconventional faith which began in this early period. Intimately connected to her discovery of self was her discovery of God. This second and deeper dimension of her inner journey became the mainstay of her life, holding her, and freeing her to care amid the despair and cruelty of the camp.

The third chapter explored her struggle against hatred which continues through the whole span of her diaries and letters, from March 1941 to September 1943 when she boarded the train to Auschwitz. From the beginning, her stand against this 'sickness of the soul' only deepened in intensity, as paradoxically the reasons to hate grew stronger. Part of her strategy was not to be afraid.

Through the winter of 1941 and early months of 1942, while

others became desperate to flee or hide, Etty cycled and walked through the streets and alongside the canals of Amsterdam, determined to live. For much of the time her life was extraordinarily free of the anxieties that so besieged others. She was less troubled by depressions, and her days focused on her explorations in literature, her studies of Russian and her wide range of friendships. Underneath everything was her growing awareness of her inner life that was becoming ever more important to her. And through all this period she was immersed in a relationship with Spier which encompassed all these things.

This relative calm was partly because the restrictions against the Jews thus far had touched her little personally. Not that she did not care, nor for one single minute did she 'fool herself about the gravity of it all'.[1] But as a young single woman she was able to stand back and see what was happening from a wider, more detached perspective. She was determined not to allow her mind to become poisoned by the all-pervasive hatred and fear. And so, in this mid-period of the diaries, references to the persecution are scattered, its horror kept at bay.

## July 1942 – a shift in focus

All this changes at the beginning of the tenth book of the diary. In early July 1942, the mood of her writing alters. The pace quickens. In response to the rising intensity of the persecution, there is a noticeable shift in focus. There is no alternative but to face what is coming.

Before we look at how she faced it, we need to try to comprehend what was happening in the wider picture, try to grasp the full import and horror.

In the months after May 1940, at the beginning of the German occupation of Holland, it might have been possible to believe that life for the large Jewish population of Amsterdam would continue relatively normally, notwithstanding the ravages and insecurities of a wider European and world war. Initially things were relatively calm, and life, even for the Jews, continued much as before.

But during 1941 things started to deteriorate and slowly but surely the noose began to tighten. There were raids on Jewish businesses, and a series of restrictions and exclusions began to be put in place. What was to come started to show its ugly face.

But it was not until 1942 that the persecution developed on such a scale that ordinary life for the Jewish population began to become impossible. The driving force behind this came from the Wannsee conference on the 'Final Solution' held in Berlin in January 1942. This conference

ushered in the final stage of escalation of the extermination policy – the incorporation of the whole of German-occupied Europe in a comprehensive programme of systematic annihilation of the Jews. The evolution of such a programme, once initiated as a planned operation, rapidly gathered pace in the spring . . .[2]

As the intensity of the persecution accelerated and the hatred became focused in an unremitting barrage of restrictions and measures, it became clear to the Jews of Amsterdam, beyond any possibility of doubt, that the Nazis were intent on their destruction.

## A barrage of restrictions

In March all Jewish funds in Dutch banks had to be transferred to the one bank of Lippman, Rosenthal and Company. At the end of April it was decreed that all Jews must wear a yellow star when going out. From May a German office took over the issuing of travel permits to Jews and far fewer were issued. During this period Jewish movements were increasingly restricted: they were forbidden from entering cafes, libraries or swimming baths, they were no longer allowed to go onto beaches or swim in the sea, and everywhere signs reading 'Jews not allowed', or 'Jews not welcome' began to appear. In June rumours began to circulate that all Jews were to be deported out of Holland.

On 22nd June Jews across Holland were ordered to hand in their bicycles (20th July in Amsterdam). On 30th June, a catalogue of restrictions came into force curtailing movement and isolating Jews from the wider population and from one another: Jews had be in their homes from 8pm to 6am; Jews were not to stay in the dwellings of non-Jews; Jews could only buy in non-Jewish shops between 3pm and 5pm; the delivery of articles to Jewish homes was forbidden; Jews could not enter non-Jewish barber shops or other paramedical establishments; Jews could not enter railways stations or use trams, buses or any private transport. Finally, Jews were not allowed to use the public phone system and so their phones were cut off.

## Mass deportation

These restrictions, aimed at isolating, demoralizing and humiliating the Jews, were the prelude to mass deportation. In July 1942, the systematic removal of all Jews from Amsterdam to Camp Westerbork began. Westerbork ceased to be a refugee camp and became a *Juden-durchgangslager* – a transit camp for Jews on their way to labour and concentration camps in the east. On 15th July, the first deportation train left Westerbork. The trains were destined for Auschwitz or Sobibor, or sometimes Bergen-Belsen and Theresienstadt. A systematic process on a vast scale of moving large numbers of human beings to their death went into operation. The ultimate aim was to pronounce Holland 'Judenfrei'.

## Etty's response

How did Etty respond to all this? We have already noted two kinds of response. She found herself driven to her knees and taken deeper into her practice of praying and silence. Her body became a kind of sanctuary, her own secret convent cell with its high protective walls drawn round it. Here she shielded and nourished the flame of her inner life.

And she formed the resolute conviction that in the face of such hatred and suffering the only creative response that a person could make if their humanity is to survive is to learn to bear it, to make 'a decent shelter' for their sorrow.

But in the diary entries of the month of July 1942, as the onslaught began to intensify with a terrible ferocity, she writes of a yet deeper response – a going further even than learning 'to bear sorrow'. On the face of it, it seems utterly negative.

## Acceptance

She writes of the need totally to *accept*, *absorb* and even *embrace* the future of death and destruction which cannot be avoided. The huge and impossible challenge which she faced – which she believes they all faced – was actively to prepare for it, to anticipate it, even mentally to rehearse it . . . in every possible way fully to absorb it . . . *so, when it does come, they will not be overwhelmed by it.*

On 3rd July sitting at her desk, she writes: 'What is at stake is our impending destruction and annihilation; we can have no more illusions about that. They are out to destroy us completely, *we must accept that and go on from there*'[3] (my italics).

But how, the mind asks, can a person possibly 'go on from there'?

'Today I was filled with a terrible despair', she writes. But then she rallies adding, '. . . and I shall have to come to terms with that as well.' The only way to deal with that also, is *acceptance*.

As she struggles to comprehend what it means totally and without any qualification to accept the negative, she senses that it is somehow a step forward.

An awful lot has happened inside me these last few days, something has crystallised. I have looked our destruction, our miserable end . . . straight in the eye, and accepted it into my life. And my love of life has not been diminished.[4]

There is a note of surprise, even amazement in her as she states the seemingly impossible paradox: 'I continue to grow from day to day with the likelihood of destruction staring me in the face.'

The realization of imminent violent death is a terrible thing for a human being to absorb. But coming to terms with it, she believed, was crucial. 'What matters', she writes, 'is that we are all marked men.' She believed that that must be fully grasped if, paradoxically, the prospect of death was not to destroy them. So she came to realize that death – even the kind they will face – has to be greeted, not feared.

## 'My life has . . . been extended by death'

Etty writes of her death as a kind of companion she is getting used to. 'I greet him', she says, 'as an old acquaintance . . . There death suddenly stands, having slipped simply, unmistakably and almost silently into my life. He has a place in it now, and I know that he is part of it.'

As she looks him straight in the eye she finds that her life, far from being diminished is, extraordinarily, enriched.

> My life, has, so to speak, been extended by death, by my looking death in the eye and accepting it, by accepting destruction as part of life and no longer wasting my energies on fear of death or the refusal to acknowledge its inevitability.[5]

By facing up to it, she begins to find freedom from the power of it. But merely to state it is not enough. This end, this path to 'annihilation', has to be imagined and mentally rehearsed. They must think through and absorb the detail of how it will be.

One day she and Spier have to visit the tax office. Because they cannot use the trams, they need to walk – and it is a long way. She is exhausted with blisters on her feet. She writes:

> During our walk I knew that a house was waiting for us at the end, but I also knew that a time would come when there would

be nothing like that and all our walks would end in some barracks . . . and I accepted that too.[6]

In her determination to follow this radical way of acceptance she is strengthened by a sense of identification with others down the centuries who have similarly suffered. As the two of them trudge down Amsterdam's long streets, with trams going by on which they are not allowed to travel, passing pavement cafés where they are prohibited from sitting, she becomes aware of countless others through the ages who 'have been tired and have worn their feet out on God's earth in the cold and the heat . . .' 'I am not alone in my tiredness or sickness or fears,' she writes, 'but at one with millions of others from many centuries, and it is all part of life . . .'

Part of her acceptance is a greater self-acceptance, of her physical weakness and limits, something she has found difficult to acknowledge before. She tells herself: 'You're in a poor state Etty, your body is completely unfit and has no resistance; in a labour camp you'd break down inside three days.'

## 'Everything that came storming at me'

As she embraces everything they face, determined to exclude nothing and accept 'life as one indivisible whole', she is like some kind of prize fighter in training. Though physically weak, mentally she daily grows stronger, as she prepares to take on a terrible foe. A week later she writes:

Yet once more I was able to brave it all, everything that came storming at me, and now I can bear a little more than I was able to bear yesterday . . . even the moments of deepest sadness and black despair finally make me stronger.[7]

The battle is for her own heart, to keep herself alive within. Alive and spacious and caring, still able to laugh and live and love and not be overcome, not be numbed by despair, or 'shrivel up with the bitter-ness of it all'.

Perhaps the most poignant of her many anticipations of the future in this vivid July 1942 diary is when she imagines the call-up card to go to Westerbork arriving. As she mentally prepares, she is like a young explorer kitting herself out for some great expedition into the unknown that will test every bit of her – mind, soul and body – to the uttermost.

Suppose the card came tomorrow; how would I act then? I wouldn't tell a soul at first but retire to the quietest spot in the house, withdraw into myself and gather what strength I could from every cranny of my body and soul. I would have my hair cut short and throw my lipstick away. I would try to finish reading the Rilke letters before the week was out. And I'd have a pair of trousers and a jacket made out of that heavy winter coat material I've got left over. I would try to see my parents of course and do my best to reassure them, and every spare minute I would want to write to him, to the man I shall always long for ... In a few days' time I shall go to the dentist and have lots and lots of holes in my teeth filled. For that really would be awful: suffering from toothache out there. I shall try to get hold of a rucksack and pack only what is absolutely essential, though everything must be of good quality. I shall take a Bible along and that slim volume *Letters to a Young Poet*, and surely I'll be able to find some corner for the *Book of Hours*. I won't take along any photographs of those I love; I'll just take all the faces and familiar gestures I have collected and hang them up along the walls of my inner space so that they will always be with me. And these two hands will go along with me, their expressive fingers like strong young twigs. And these hands will keep pro-tecting me in prayer and will not leave me till the end. And these dark eyes will go with me, with their benign gentle, questing look.[8]

In her imagination all she really needs are clothes to keep her warm; books to nourish her inner life – just the Bible and Rilke; the faces and gestures of others hung along the walls of her inner space; her hands to protect her in prayer, and her eyes – with their 'benign gentle questing look' – to enable her to fulfil her mission of seeing.

## Greater and greater simplicity

Nothing else is needed. The period of July 1942 onwards was a time for shedding everything. In the face of the coming suffering her search was for greater and greater simplicity. All surplus baggage of the mind, of the heart, as well as surplus things must be jettisoned. Life must be stripped down to its bare essentials.

As she prepares for what is so grossly *un*civilized, she is aware of doing things for the last time, bidding farewell to what has been familiar and civilized:

> Every pretty blouse I put on is a kind of celebration. And so is every occasion I have to wash with scented soap in a bathroom all to myself for half an hour. It's as if I were revelling in these civilised luxuries for the last time.[9]

But it is not just comfort and her delight in being feminine and clean that she must shed. For Etty, one of the greatest blocks to people's capacity to deal creatively with the situation they face is the danger of succumbing to illusion, which only pitches people into weakness and desperation as they clutch at false hopes. In July 1942 many in the Jewish Council cling to the hope that the British may land. Etty accurately assesses the likelihood of this when she says: 'I believe that we must rid ourselves of all expectations of help from the outside world.'[10] A ruthless determination to face up to reality on all fronts was part of her preparation. This too was part of the stripping down.

## 'We must just be'

As she journeys further into an attitude of radical non-attachment there is a kind of Buddhist severity which takes her deeper into simplicity. 'With each minute that passes', she writes, 'I shed more wishes and desires and attachments.' 'We have to rid ourselves of . . . all sense of security, find the courage to let go of everything . . .'[11]

Even words may need to be left behind. Etty loved words, and yet as she faces up to being sent to a concentration camp beyond Westerbork when the survival of her humanity as well as her life will be at stake, then words and explanations will reach the end of their power. 'Such words as "god" and "death" and "suffering" and "eternity" are best forgotten. We have to become as simple and wordless as the growing corn or the falling rain. We must just be.'[12]

What she was straining forward to find and hold onto was a radical simplicity and purity of heart so that she would not become prey to fear; so that evil would not get any kind of hold on her; so that no evil *in* her could be touched and aroused by the evil being done *to* her.

> One moment it is Hitler, the next it is Ivan the Terrible; one moment it is Inquisition and the next war, pestilence, earthquake, or famine. Ultimately what matters most is to bear the pain, to cope with it, and to keep a small corner of one's soul unsullied, come what may.[13]

'. . . to keep a small corner of one's soul *unsullied*'. She knows that if she can do that they will have no power over her. She will not become their victim. She will not be reduced by them.

And her death will be her choice. A choice to share her people's suffering.

## A common destiny

There is an entry of 8th July 1942 in which she writes of her deliberate choice to share the 'common destiny' of her people. She writes of strapping her share of this destiny tightly on her back until it becomes part of her, as though it is some kind of tightly fitting rucksack in which a great burden is carried and which fits so tightly that it even becomes part of her body. Her sense of identification with her people is that strong. 'And that part of our common destiny that I must shoulder myself; I strap it tightly and firmly to my back, it becomes part of me as I walk through the streets even now.'[14] As she walks through the shattered city, past the houses and businesses of people she has known who have disappeared or been shot or imprisoned, she shares some small part of their loss and agony. It is a '*common* destiny'.

But in one phrase here the English translation does not fully capture the possible meaning of her original Dutch. Where the English translation is simply, 'it becomes part of me', the Dutch word she uses, '*vergroei*', carries the meaning of becoming *misshapen* as she becomes more and more identified with this burden. So her sentence could be translated: '. . . as I strap it ever more tightly and firmly to my back [her part of their common destiny], and it becomes part of me, I *grow out of shape* with it, or, am *deformed* by it'.

As one ponders the image of this young Jewish woman picking up and strapping to her shoulder a burden so heavy and ugly that its weight and outline deforms her as she walks through the streets, for the reader of the New Testament it is difficult not to catch a glimpse of another Jew, on another street, bearing the burden of a destiny which 'deformed' him.

## Why didn't she hide?

Etty's commitment to sharing her people's destiny goes some way to explaining one of the most vexed questions that surrounds her story

– why didn't she hide? It was not that she did not have plenty of chances. It is a question which people have asked since, and which many of her friends asked then.

Across Europe something like 25,000 Jews went into hiding during the Second World War. Hiding was not easy. It required a suitable place, the support of non-Jewish friends who were prepared to risk their lives either to hide you or to assist with supplies from the outside world, and it required money. The most famous person who hid was the young Dutch Jewish girl Anne Frank who, together with her father and mother and sister, went into hiding on 6th July 1942 in a secret annexe at the back of the building her father's firm occupied in a side street beside a canal just off one of Amsterdam's main thoroughfares. With the exception of her father Otto, the Frank family and those who hid with them did not survive the war. The annexe was raided by the Nazis on 4th August 1944 and the family was sent to Westerbork and then they went on the final train that left for Auschwitz on 3rd September 1944. Anne and her sister Margot eventually died in Bergen-Belsen in March 1945, both of them having contracted typhoid.

The Frank family did not succeed in their attempt to hide, but others – something like 18,000 out of a total of 25,000 – did. Although it was a tiny number when set against the six million Jews who died, it nevertheless shows that hiding held out a real possibility of survival.

On several occasions Etty was offered this possibility and promise, but repeatedly she refused to consider it. It was not as though – had she agreed – she would have been going against the views of those around her. To hide, and survive, was regarded as a moral duty if a person had the contacts and resources needed. She writes: 'Many accuse me of indifference and passivity when I refuse to go into hiding; they say that I have given up. They say everyone who can must try to stay out of their clutches, it's our bounden duty to try.'[15]

But she would not try. Despite repeated attempts to persuade her by those who knew her well and could see how much she had to offer the world, she would not agree to it.

Her friend Lenie Wolff, whose father had been a teaching colleague with Louis Hillesum, and so had known Etty since her childhood, and who herself went into hiding and survived the war, tried desperately to persuade her. Her friend and former lover Klaas Smelik and members of his family also tried. Klaas's sister offered her a hiding place, and in February 1943 Klaas himself with his daughter Jopie, a friend of Etty, planned to 'kidnap' her and hide her in their house in Hilversum. She removed herself out of the way in time. But Smelik would not give up easily. On another occasion, when she was about to leave for Westerbork, he tried to grab her and convince her of the danger she faced. Again she refused. Finally, in Westerbork itself there were those who had experienced the barbarity of Nazi imprisonment – who knew what it was really like. They tried to persuade her. She would have none of it.

All these efforts were to no avail. She was resolute in refusing the idea of hiding. Why was she so adamant in view of what was almost certainly going to happen to her?

There are perhaps three reasons, which speak of the person she was – or had become.

First, it was a matter of solidarity. She had a profound sense that she belonged to the whole Jewish community. She could no longer think of her life in terms of herself as an individual on her own. They shared a *common* destiny, and she could not absent herself from that. Perhaps the deepest thing she had discovered in her spiritual journey was that the secret of life is its inter-connectedness. She belonged to others, and others belonged to her. She had discovered that she truly lived insofar as the deepest and best in her was in communion with the deepest and best in others. This is what she had learnt to 'hearken for' – expressed in the German word she uses, '*hineinhorchen*', the meaning of which, when she uses it again towards the end of the diary, she extends even further: 'the most essential and the deepest in me hearkening unto the most essential and deepest in the other. God to God.'[16]

So in a very real sense she had lost individual 'self-interest'. If others had to go, she was not interested in saving herself. It is as though she identified with others to such an extent that egoism had dissolved in her. To think of separating herself off, therefore, as others were urging her to do, and silently hiding away from the destiny that thousands of her fellow Jews were facing, was inconceivable.

But passions fly when the subject comes up. In one passage of the diary she goes over the arguments again. As she writes, one can hear the impassioned voices of her friends pleading with her, accusing her, berating her. It is one of the most revealing passages of her writing. Her argument with them takes her to the very roots of her self where she knows she may face the final testing. Only then will she know the final answer to her own question about what kind of person she ultimately is.

People often get worked up when I say it doesn't really matter whether I go or somebody else does, the main thing is that so many thousands *have* to go. It is not as if I want to fall into the arms of destruction with a resigned smile – far from it. I am only bowing to the inevitable, and even as I do so I am sustained by the certain knowledge that ultimately they cannot rob us of anything that matters. I certainly do not want to go out of some sort of masochism, to be torn away from what has been the basis of my existence these last few years. But I don't think I would feel happy if I were exempted from what so many others have to suffer. They keep telling me that someone like me has a duty to go into hiding because I have so many things to do in life, so much to give. But I know that whatever I may have to give to others, I can give it no matter where I am, here in the circle of my friends or over there, in a concentration camp. And it is sheer arrogance to think oneself too good to share the fate of the masses. And if God Himself should feel that I still have a great deal to do, well then, I shall do it after I have suffered what all the others have to suffer. And whether or not I am a valuable human being will become clear only from my behaviour in more arduous circumstances. And if I should not survive, how I die will show me who I really am.[17]

A second reason was because of fear. To go into hiding would mean to become afraid. She associated hiding with fear – with people saying in their terror we must not 'let them get us into their clutches'. And she had seen what fear does: how it eviscerates the soul. She continued to wage a battle against the power of fear in her own heart and she knew that if she went into hiding, fearful every day that she might be found, she would lose that battle and would 'shrivel up', her soul invaded by fear – and in a sense, she would die.

The third reason was to do with her sense of vocation. Through her time with Spier and her writing of her diary, she had come to use and understand her gifts – both with people and with words. In the end, far from trying to get away from Westerbork, this led to her actually *wanting* to go there – wanting to be at the forefront of life where people were hurting and where she could use her skills to relieve some of that pain – and tell the story of their fate. It was, as we shall see, a twofold vocation fundamental to her identity.

The seeds of all these reasons had germinated in her heart many months before the crisis time of the summer of 1942. Over the months with Spier she had emerged as a different kind of person with different kinds of understandings and priorities. It is no wonder that her past lover and friend Klaas Smelik could not understand her. On the last occasion that he tried in vain to persuade her to hide, there was a physical struggle in which he grasped hold of her, trying again to convince her of the danger she faced. Smelik recounts the occasion:

> She wormed herself free and stood at a distance of about five feet from me. She looked at me very strangely and said, 'You don't understand me.' I replied: 'No, I don't understand what on earth you're up to. Why don't you stay here, you fool!' Then she said: 'I want to share the destiny of my people.' When she said that, I knew there was no hope. She would never come to us.[18]

But the cost of not hiding was to remain exposed.

## Life coming to an end

The new regulations of 30th June made her particularly exposed. One of the restrictions was that Jews could not live in the same houses as non-Jews. So her position in Han Wegerif's house became precarious. In fact an exception was allowed when residence was necessary upon the grounds of existing rental or labour contracts. So she could remain as housekeeper, but she could not know how long this would last. 'Perhaps I shall be able to stay on here for another month,' she writes, 'but by that time any loophole in the regulations will surely have been closed.'[19] Her situation was very insecure – and all around her in the swollen, crowded streets of the Jewish communities, life was disintegrating. She struggled to anticipate what this will mean – for others and herself. How will she cope with being torn away from those she loves? Her meetings with Spier are full of sadness – 'every encounter is also a farewell'.[20] And what others are going through and what they had yet to face is always in her mind:

> We still have to go through a great deal. We shall become poor, then destitute, until in the end our strength will go, not only because of all the fears and uncertainties but also, very simply, because we are banned from more and more shops and therefore have to cover longer distances on foot, which is already undermining the health of many people I know. From all sides our destruction creeps up on us and soon the ring will be closed and no one at all will be able to come to our aid.[21]

## Dissociation and despair

However, despite all this, she feels remarkably calm – even 'strangely happy' with 'a new gentleness and a new confidence growing stronger inside me . . .' But she wonders about the degree of her detachment, her dissociation: 'I don't know how to put it, it is as if I had gone almost too far in my dissociation from all that drives most people out of their minds.'[22]

But she is not always so detached. Only the night before, she had spent the evening with Han Wegerif with whom she had lived for the last five years. She writes of how, in the darkness, the walls keeping her despair locked up inside her come tumbling down. It is at a moment of the most intense life that the floodgates open within her and she weeps, *owning* her sorrow.

> . . . when we talked before an open window about the latest developments and I looked into his tortured face, I had the feeling: tonight we shall lie in each other's arms and sob. We did indeed lie in each other's arms but we did not sob. Only when his body lay above mine in our final ecstasy did a flood tide of despair, of elemental human sorrow, rise up from deep within me and submerge me, and there was so much pity for myself and for everyone else . . . in the dark I was able to bury my head between his naked shoulders and weep my tears in secret.[23]

## Everything put to the test

Through these days of July, under the onslaught of this despair, everything she has learnt over the last 18 months is put to the test. The disciplines she has learnt to practise steady her. As she struggles to cope with the overcrowding, she finds she needs solitude: 'I have to be alone so much.'[24] As they begin to be robbed of every outer thing, she searches out inner space: 'There is always a quiet room in some corner of our being and we can always retire there for a while. Surely they can't rob us of that.'[25] And at her beloved desk – 'where rose petals now lie scattered among her books' – she cherishes silence: 'there is a vast silence in me, that continues to grow'.[26]

Then there is a time of particular testing. She receives a summons to report to Westerbork. She greets this mostly with a profound calm – a 'great sense of surrender . . . to everything that is to come'. She tells herself that she can stand up to 'this bit of history'. But then she describes succumbing, momentarily, to a kind of deathly disintegration, as though she is being seized by a terrible fear:

> . . . sometimes I feel as if a layer of ashes were being sprinkled over my heart, as if my face were withering and decaying before my very eyes, and as if everything were falling apart in front of me and my heart were letting everything go.[27]

But these are only moments. The next day, after another spell of despair she writes, 'No, I don't think I shall perish.'[28] She realizes that it is not possible to anticipate everything, life has to be lived through, it cannot be just imagined.

> A few days ago I thought that nothing more could happen to me, that I had suffered everything in anticipation, but today I suddenly realized that things can indeed weigh more heavily on me than ever I thought possible. And they were very, very heavy . . .

As the trough of despair passes, the disciplined part of her mind asserts itself again and she tells herself:

> It is good to have such moments of despair and temporary extinction; continuous calm would be superhuman. But now I know that I shall always get the better of despair. This afternoon I should not have thought it possible that, by this evening, I would be so calm again . . . I know that I shall often lie broken and ruined, crushed against God's earth. But I also believe I'm quite tough, and that I shall always be able to get up again.

She is faced with very practical questions – this time for real. Her friend Jopie Smelik comes and 'like a second St Martin' takes off her wool sweater which wards off the rain and the cold and gives it to

Etty. 'Just the garment', she says, 'for a long journey.'[29] She wonders if, among her blankets, she can squeeze in her Russian Dictionaries and Dostoyevsky's novel, *The Idiot*, along with food, though she feels that books are more important than food. Later in the day she remembers Dostoyevsky in prison in Siberia for four years, 'never allowed to be alone', with only the Bible to read, and terrible sanitary conditions. And all the time she thinks of Spier, and being with him and leaving him, and his weakness and need.

## 'Dear God, what will happen to me?'

Then there is another stab of fear. She tells of a brief conversation about the camp she has that same day with her friend Werner Levie who warns her that life in a camp only hardens and brutalizes people. 'You mustn't imagine there are lots of "spiritual advantages" to be gained in that kind of camp', he says, in a rather crushing way. 'You grow a "hard shell" round you, that's all.' Etty knows that for her that simply won't work. 'A hard shell won't fit me; I shall remain defence-less and open to everything.'[30]

Suddenly she is very afraid: 'Dear God, what will happen to me?' she writes. Then she adds, 'No, I shall not ask You beforehand, I shall bear every moment, even the most unimaginable . . .' As we read her words, it is not difficult to sense her mind spinning with real panic.

## The Jewish Council

In fact she did not go. The next day she was appointed to the Jewish Council which gave some protection against the immediate threat of deportation. She had been urged by her brother Jaap to apply for work there, and due to the mediation of a high-ranking member she was rapidly appointed. She felt uncomfortable about the letter of application as though she had done something underhand 'like crowding onto a small piece of wood adrift on an endless ocean after a shipwreck and then saving oneself by pushing others into the water and watching them drown'. She adds: 'I would much rather join those who prefer to float on their backs for a while, drifting on the ocean with their eyes turned towards heaven, and who then go down with a prayer.'[31]

But it meant that she was able to stay on in Amsterdam. She worked as a secretary doing administrative duties – and disliked it intensely.

But still the dread of call-up was there. A day comes when she thinks her call-up notice has arrived:

> This morning I found a buff envelope in my letter box, I could see there was a white paper inside. I was quite calm and thought, 'My call-up notice, what a pity, now I won't have time to try repacking my rucksack.' Later I noticed that my knees were shaking.[32]

In fact it was not the call-up but simply a form for the Jewish Council staff to fill in, but she reflects: 'I am still tied by a thousand threads to everything I treasure here.'

Of all the threads that tie her, most of all she fears losing her home, and the oasis of her beloved desk. In her prayer she says: '. . . I must make You a candid confession: if I have to leave this house I shall be totally lost.' And she prays: 'Take these worries from me, please, for if I have to bear them as well as all the others, I shall scarcely be able to go on living.' It seems that her prayers are answered, for a few lines later her tone is different as the direction in which her deepest self is leading her becomes clear: '. . . I am grateful to You for driving me from my peaceful desk into the midst of the cares and sufferings of this age. It wouldn't do, would it, to live an idyllic life with You in a sheltered study?' And she adds: 'I am deeply grateful to You for leaving me so free of bitterness and hate, with so much calm acceptance.' [33]

## 'I say my goodbyes from minute to minute'

Anxiety, fear, confidence, trust – they are all part of her fragile vulnerability as slowly her ties with the world of Amsterdam, which she so loves, loosen. A week before she goes to Westerbork for the first time she writes: 'I say my goodbyes from minute to minute, shaking myself free of all outer things. I cut through the ropes that still hold me bound, I load everything I need to set out on my journey.'

She is calm, sad, resolute – and frightened. What will the future hold for her, what will it do not just to her body but to her spirit? 'I am sitting now beside a quiet canal, my legs dangling over the stone wall, and I wonder whether one day my heart will be so weary and worn that it will no longer fly where it wants, free as a bird.'[34]

And then at the end of the month, at her own request, she is transferred to the department of social work at Westerbork. But before she goes, there is a final episode in this self-emptying part of her story to be gone through. One final rope to cut.

## Spier

Through all this month of July, Spier is increasingly weak and ill with lung cancer and not far from death. His deteriorating condition gives this summer of 1942, when she faces up to the loss of so much, a particularly personal edge.

Yet in the end, leaving him is not so difficult. As she senses her growing inner strength and sees him beginning to fade, she knows that she can move on from him. Their roles are now reversed. On one occasion when the few minutes they can find together have passed and she is going, he becomes desperate: 'You must not go from me, you must stay.'[35]

The next day she returns, and as she sits beside his sick-bed he mentions the idea of them getting married – even at this late stage – as a way of staying together, though he immediately puts the idea away. Later that evening she writes:

All sorts of things are becoming clear to me. For instance, this: I don't want to be S's wife . . . He is an old man whom I love, love infinitely, and to whom I shall always be united by an inner bond. But 'marry' . . . I must in all seriousness and honesty say finally that I do not want to. And the fact that I am going to go my own way all by myself gives me a great feeling of strength.[36]

## Westerbork

And she does go her own way. On 30th July, two days later, she goes to Westerbork for the first time, to work in 'Social Welfare for People in Transit'. After so much trepidation, she enters the world that had loomed so threateningly. She was in a privileged position for the time being and exempt from the transport trains, but she could not know how long that would last. She faced the world she had feared, and strangely, she was set free.

In this new role of social welfare worker she was able to travel to and from the camp. She was not yet an internee. Her first visit there lasted just two weeks. On 14th August she was back in Amsterdam for a few days, and on the 19th she went to Deventer for the last time, to see her parents. Around 21st August she returned to Westerbork. Then Spier died on 15th September. By then she was back in Amsterdam, beginning to suffer from illness which obliged her to stay there for most of the winter and spring of 1942 and 1943.

## A released person

The last section of the diary – exercise book 11 – lasts from 15th September to 13th October 1942. In it Etty is a released person. Although her illness begins to trouble her, nevertheless the tone of her writing is different from the agonies of the month of July. Why? She was the other side of her fears of Westerbork; she had faced up to her death; she had radically simplified her life; she had left behind what she thought she could not do without; and she had a new role and purpose where her gifts could be used.

And Spier had died. This was a release for him – at the end he was in terrible pain, and the day after he died the Gestapo came for him. And release for her too – not that she was not profoundly grateful. Before her diary ends there are many references to his memory, full of gratitude. She remembers again that he was the one 'who had attended at the birth of my soul',[37] and in retrospect she is able to see him clearly – both his greatness and his obvious imperfections – a sign that she was truly free of him. With great affection, she calls him a 'dear spoiled man' and writes: 'All the bad and all the good that can be found in a man were in you – all the demons, all the passions, all the goodness, all the love – great discerner, God-seeker, and God-finder that you were.'[38]

## Sickness

Though she is back in Amsterdam, her heart is in Westerbork. But it is to be a long and frustrating winter. Other than two weeks at the end of November and the beginning of December when she returns, she is forced to remain in Amsterdam suffering from sickness – eventually gallstones are diagnosed. During this time, most of her letters are to her new friend in Westerbork, Osias Kormann. She writes to him that she longs to return to the 'great moral task' before them, but, 'giddy and weak' and in pain, it is impossible.[39] After mid-October too there is no diary. It seems she simply has to rest and wait and try to get better.

During the spring her health improves, and by May she feels well enough to go, and waits anxiously for her call-up from the Jewish Council. She hears that 15 volunteers will be needed to replace 15 who are getting leave, and she is keen to be one of them. On the evening of 5th June 1943 she writes a farewell note to her friend Maria Tuinzing, and then the next morning she leaves Amsterdam for the last time, never to return.

## A twofold vocation

Surrounded in this camp by so many 'bundles of human misery, desperate and unable to face life',[40] she felt that she had what was needed for the huge task of giving support: a deep well of compassion in her heart, and skills in the art of listening. At the heart of her vocation to care was her confidence in the inner meaning she had found.

The psychotherapist Viktor Frankl, who survived Auschwitz, has written that in such extremes, when everything is stripped away, people can only survive if they have discovered meaning.

Etty saw the people around her as empty and haunted by fear, with nothing in them to hold them in their terror, and she longed to help them find the depth of meaning that she had discovered herself. In a vivid image, she likened people to empty houses with their doors wide open: 'I walk in and roam through passages and rooms, and every house is furnished a little differently, and yet they are all of them the same . . . so many empty houses, and I shall prepare them all for You, the most honoured lodger.'[41]

But there was an even more compelling vocation. Over the months, as she had practised her talent with words and realized her capacity to 'read people'; and as she had felt again and again a deep moral outrage at what was being done to them, the conviction grew in her that she *must* write. '. . . if I have one real duty in life, in these times, at this stage of my life, then it is to write, to record, to retain'.[42] She will be the chronicler. 'At this moment I know, more certainly than ever, that I have a task in this life, a small project specially for me. And I shall have to live through everything . . . I shall become the chronicler of our adventures.'[43]

Her pen will be the instrument with which she will fight this evil. But the material of their lives is hard and brutal and the story unyielding – it does not wish to be told in all its awfulness. She likens herself to a blacksmith possessed of a kind of elemental passion:

And I shall wield this slender fountain pen as if it were a hammer, and my words will have to be so many hammer strokes with which to beat out the story of our fate and of a piece of history as it is and never was before. Not in this totalitarian, massively organised form, spanning the whole of Europe.[44]

In this task of chronicling, her greatest fear was numbness. If she is to see beyond the surface of things, she must remain alive in her heart, in touch with her own quicksilver life, always able to 'hearken' to herself, to others and to God. Numbness is to be feared because it will block her off from her inner sources, and prevent her from fulfilling her most compelling task which is to 'bear witness'. 'What I fear most is numbness', she writes, 'And yet' – and in one sentence she sums up her deepest passion: '... *there must be someone to live through it all and bear witness to the fact that God lived, even in these times*'[45] (my italics).

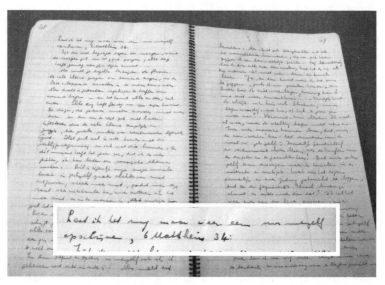

Two pages of the diary of 29th September 1942; inset: 'Just let me write it out once more for myself, 6 Matthew 34:'

*Patrick Woodhouse*

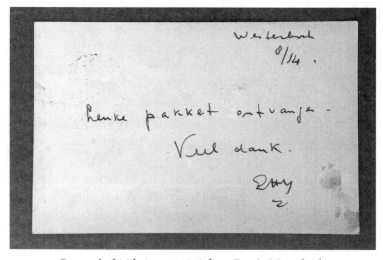

Postcard of 14th August 1943 from Etty in Westerbork.
'Nice packet received. Many thanks. Etty'

*Reinhard Conings*

# Chapter 5

# Seeing Differently

*These dark eyes will go with me with their benign gentle quest-
ing look.*

If, today, you visit the site of the camp where Etty Hillesum spent the
last months of her life, you will discover a quiet and peaceful place.

At the entrance to the site there is a small museum among the pine
trees which tells the story of Camp Westerbork. On most weekdays
during school term it is full of parties of Dutch schoolchildren
coming to learn about the place where, during the darkest days of the
Second World War, more than 100,000 Dutch Jews were held by the
Nazis before being taken on trains to their death in the east.

The site of the camp itself cannot be reached by car. It is kept as
a secluded space, a further three kilometres on into the woods.
The visitor may walk there or catch the little bus from outside the
museum which makes its way through the forest and stops outside
the gate of what is now a wide piece of open ground half a kilometre
square.

As you walk through the gate, between the barbed-wire fence that
still stands on each side, you will see that almost all the buildings that
made up Camp Westerbork are now gone, torn down after the war.
Only the outer structure of a few still remain – gaunt reminders of
the rows of barracks that once stood there during the worst years of
the twentieth century, housing tens of thousands of desperate people
in intolerable conditions.

Near the centre of the site is a stone memorial with a text from the book of Psalms inscribed on it, 'My sorrow is continually before me'. But at one side, near to the barbed-wire perimeter fence and a solitary watchtower, there is another, more poignant memorial of what happened here: 50 metres of the original railway track which took the trains, with their helpless human cargo to the east, still remain. At one end are buffers, and at the other the rails themselves are torn up and twisted skywards as if to say, never again.

It was to this barren patch of heath near to the German border that Etty Hillesum first came at the end of July 1942, as a staff member of the Jewish Council, to give support to those who had been hunted down and forced to leave their homes, and were now 'in transit' to labour or concentration camps in Germany and Poland.

## Letters about Westerbork

The letters which Etty wrote about Westerbork convey a vivid picture of what the Nazi Holocaust actually meant in terms of human suffering. Through the gift of her writing, the terrible reality of what happened there was exposed, forcing the question again: how could human beings be capable of doing such things?

What is it about her writing that makes it so powerful? And what does her writing tell us about her as a person – who she was, and how she had changed?

The first thing that strikes the reader is that – given the nature of her subject – she writes with a remarkable degree of emotional detachment.

It is not that she did not feel passionately about the people and issues of Westerbork, but over the weeks and months in Amsterdam, during which the storm of anti-semitism had raged around her, she had very largely dealt with her own fear and despair. And so she was able to *see clearly*, her vision unclouded by her own pain and distress.

In the letters there is remarkably little about herself in terms of her inner feelings. This may be partly because the letters were not private documents as her diaries were. But it may also be because, although Westerbork brought her face to face with new horrors, by and large there was little which she had not already seen, and suffered, and consciously absorbed. Her path of acceptance had been a constant battle, and continued to be so, but on the whole she had done the work; she had faced her fear, and she had – to a considerable degree – absorbed and accepted even her own death. *And so she was free to see and look beyond herself to what was happening in the experience and struggles of others.* Rather than dwelling on her own struggles, her energy became focused on building a new and different kind of world, for she had already lived through and absorbed the grim realities of the present one.

This comes across in a letter from the camp to her old friend Klaas Smelik in which she uses a strange image:

> I shall try to convey to you how I feel . . . When a spider spins its web does it not cast the main threads ahead of itself; and then follows along them from behind? The main path of my life stretches like a long journey before me and already reaches into another world. It is just as if everything that happens here and that is still to happen were somehow discounted inside me. As if I had been through it already and was now helping to build a new and different society.[1]

She feels as though she has been 'through it already'. But not so that she has become hardened to what the terrible realities of the present world are doing to others.

Second, Etty's writing exudes compassion for those who are most vulnerable in the camp – the screaming babies, the stumbling frail and elderly, the paralyzed and disabled, the crying children and desperate mothers, those who are blind or on stretchers or can barely walk because of hunger – the whole diverse bundle of struggling humanity whom she now feels it is her role to support, with the same kind of passion and intensity that once she directed towards meeting her own needs.

A third quality, moral outrage, is there too, often expressed through bitter irony. What she sees appals her, and the force of her outrage is all the more powerful for being understated. The bare facts of cruelty, the sharp contrasts between tyrant and victim, often the bleak absurdities of the Nazi posturing: all are simply and devastatingly exposed.

Many of the letters are long and detailed, and among them are two in which she particularly warmed to her task of being the 'chronicler' of their fate. Such was the power of these two letters that they were published illegally during the war and circulated among the Dutch resistance.

## Encountering Westerbork

The first letter, which serves as an introduction to the life of the camp as it was in 1942, was written at the end of December 1942. It followed the time she had spent at Westerbork in the summer and autumn, and was written to 'two sisters in the Hague' as a result of a request from a doctor whom she had met in the camp, who asked her if she would write to his two sisters about life in Westerbork. As well as a response to his request, the letter is an extended diary for Etty herself. It tells something of the story of her own early encounter with the place, and through her descriptions we glimpse the perspective of this young woman walking with extraordinary poise into the human debris of a world where human life was regarded with contempt.

The letter begins with her arrival and she touches on the history of the place. Since 1939 Westerbork had been a camp for German Jewish refugees fleeing the Nazis.

It was the summer when I came here for the first time. Up till then, all I'd known about Drenthe was that it had a lot of megalithic tombs. And then suddenly there was a village of wooden barracks, set between heath and sky, with a glaringly yellow lupin field in the middle and barbed wire all around. And there were human lives as well, thick as flies. To be honest, I had never realised that refugees from Germany had already been held on Drenthe heath for four years . . .[2]

She tells of how she wanders round the camp in dazed amazement, meeting parts of her people's recent bitter history. 'During the first few days I walked around as if through the pages of a history book . . .' She meets people who had been 'in Buchenwald and Dachau at a time when to us these were only distant, threatening sounds'; she meets Jewish refugees who had travelled across the Atlantic and back without being allowed to disembark; she sees snapshots of children separated and lost for ever from their parents; she realizes she is glimpsing 'a small part of the Jewish predicament of the last ten years'.

And then she brings her readers up to date, for the agony of the Jews continues in this place.

In the summer of 1942 . . . this small settlement was turned upside down and shaken to the marrow. With horror, the old camp inmates witnessed the mass deportation of Jews from Holland to Eastern Europe. From the very beginning they had to make their own considerable contribution in terms of human lives when the quota of 'voluntary workers' was not completely filled.

As she tries to engage with this commission to describe the life of Westerbork now, she is at a loss to know how to begin. 'To simply record the bare facts of families torn apart, of possessions plundered and liberties forfeited, would soon become monotonous. Nor is it possible to pen picturesque accounts of barbed wire and vegetable swill to show outsiders what it's like.'

So she hesitates and ponders and then slowly builds her picture from the bare facts of the place. She begins with some of the

buildings scattered among the barracks: 'an orphanage, a synagogue, a small mortuary . . . I have heard talk of a madhouse being
built . . . and the expanding hospital barracks complex already has a
thousand beds.'

She writes of the command structure: 'We have a Dutch commandant and a German one. The first is taller, but the second has more
of a say. We are told, moreover, that he likes music and that he is a
gentleman. I'm no judge, although I must say that for a gentleman he
certainly has a somewhat peculiar job.' And she tells of the mud.
'There is mud, so much mud that somewhere between your ribs you
need to have a great deal of inner sunshine if you don't want to
become the psychological victim of it all.'

## The overcrowding

From the buildings and the 'gentleman' commandant and the mud
she moves to the chaotic diversity of the different Jewish groups
crammed into this small patch of heath.

> Although the camp buildings are all one storey, you can hear as
> many accents as if the Tower of Babel had been erected in our
> midst: Bavaria and Groningen, Saxony and Limburg, the Hague
> and East Friesland; you can hear German with a Polish accent
> and German with a Russian accent, Dutch with a German
> accent and German with a Dutch accent, Waterlooplein and
> Berlin dialects – all in an area of half a kilometre square.

The most pressing issue is the overcrowding. She tells of the 'great
waves of human beings being constantly washed in from the cities
and provinces . . . it is terribly crowded in Westerbork, as when too
many drowning people cling to the last bit of flotsam after a ship has
sunk'.

And who are these drowning people? She describes whole communities wrenched from their homes in the round-ups at night arriving

'in slippers and underclothes'; of 'slum-dwellers . . . displaying their poverty and neglect in the bare barracks'; of the Jews from Rotterdam – 'in a class by themselves' – hardened by the bombing raids; and of Jews from so many other places 'with all their rivalries . . .'

## 'Her religious sense of things'

And then she tells of a day when Jewish Catholic nuns and priests arrive. It is a particularly revealing passage. As she describes these religious seeing the cruelty and the chaos for the first time, she is speaking of herself, conveying through her account of them her own vision of the dignity of human life and the depths of her own contemplative spirit. It was this spirit that Freidrich Weinreb, an economist and Old Testament scholar who was imprisoned at the same time as Etty, noticed about her and wrote of in his memoirs: 'What I found most striking was her religious sense of things, a quality that she had recently discovered in herself. There was something about her that spoke of an ancient, primeval struggle, the weight of thousands of years – and at the same time something light and joyful.'[3]

Describing their arrival she writes:

There was a remarkable day when the Jewish Catholics or Catholic Jews – whichever you want to call them – arrived, nuns and priests wearing the yellow star on their habits. I remember two young novices, twins, with identical beautiful, dark ghetto faces and serene, childish eyes peering out from under their skullcaps. They said with mild surprise that they had been fetched at half past four in the morning from morning mass, and that they had eaten red cabbage at Amersfoort.

There was a priest, still fairly young, who had not left his monastery for fifteen years. He was out in the 'world' for the first time, and I stood next to him for a while, following his eyes as they wandered peacefully around the barracks where the newcomers were being received.

The others – shaven, beaten, maltreated – who poured in along with the Catholics that day stumbled about the wooden hut with movements that were still unsteady and stretched out their hands towards the bread, of which there was not enough.

A young Jew stood very still next to us. His jacket was much too loose, but a grin broke through his stubbly black beard when he said, 'They tried to smash the wall of the prison with my head, but my head was harder than the wall!'

Among all the shaved heads, it was strange to see the white-turbaned women who had just been treated in the delousing barracks, and who went about now looking distressed and humiliated.

Children dozed off on the dusty plank floor; others played tag among the adults. Two little ones floundered helplessly around the heavy body of a woman lying unconscious in a corner. They didn't understand why their mother just lay there without answering them.

A grey-haired old gentleman, straight as an arrow and with a clear-cut, aristocratic profile, stared at the whole infernal canvas and repeated over and over to himself: 'A terrible day! A terrible day!'

And among all this the unremitting clatter of a battery of typewriters: the machine-gun fire of bureaucracy.

. . . I looked at the priest who was now back in the world again. 'And what do you think of the world now?' I asked.

But his gaze remained unwavering and friendly above the brown habit, as if everything he saw was known, familiar from long ago.

That same evening, a man later told me, he saw some priests walking one behind the other in the dusk between two dark barracks. They were saying their rosaries as imperturbably as if they had just finished vespers at the monastery.

This powerful passage echoes her own heart, and she ends it with a question that affirms her deepest belief about human life: 'and isn't it true that one can pray anywhere, in a wooden barracks just a well as in a stone monastery, or indeed, anywhere on this earth where God, in these troubled times, feels like casting his likeness?'

## Compassion

Then she turns to the old. Here too she reveals herself. Through her descriptions of the stumbling, terrified old people who arrive in the camp, overwhelmed and confused having been violently wrenched out of what is familiar to them, we see her gentleness and compassion:

> In the history of Westerbork, surely the saddest chapter will be the one that deals with the old. . . .
> To the young and healthy, you can say something that you believe in and can act upon in your own life: that history has indeed laid a heavy destiny upon our shoulders, and that we must try to attain the grandeur we need to bear it.
> You can even say that we should consider ourselves front-line soldiers . . .
> But have you ever heard of front-line soldiers aged eighty, bearing the red-and-white canes of the blind as their weapons?

And acutely aware of the small details of their anxieties, she takes us into the inner world of the bewildered old people whom she cares for as they are unloaded from dilapidated trucks into the chaos of the barracks.

> There was a little old woman who had left her spectacles and her medicine bottle at home on the mantel – could she go and get them now, and where exactly was she, and where would she be going?

A woman of eighty-seven clung to my hand with so much strength that I thought she would never let go . . .

And the bowed little gentleman of seventy-nine: he had been married for more than fifty years, he told me; his wife was in the hospital in Utrecht, and he was about to be taken out of Holland the next day . . .

Even if I went on for pages, I still couldn't convey any idea of the shuffling and the stumbling and the falling down, the need for help along with the childish questions. You can't do much with words. A helping hand on the shoulder is sometimes too heavy.

## Shortage of space

As the round-ups from all across the Netherlands go on, she describes how space becomes the worst problem.

Of all the shortages in Westerbork concentration camp, the shortage of space is surely the worst. . . . [It] is really clear in the colossal, hastily built barracks, those jam-packed hangars of drafty slats where, under a lowering sky made up of hundreds of people's drying laundry, the iron bunks are stacked in triple decks.

. . . On these iron beds people live and die, eat, fall ill, or lie awake through the night, because so many children cry, or because they cannot help wondering why so little news comes from the thousands who have already set out from this place.

## The leading lights

Finally – in this brief survey of a long letter – she describes the 'leading lights' who, in this place of judgement, are suddenly stripped bare of all their outward armour and trappings. We are reminded of her most constant theme: that it is only what human beings have discovered and nourished within themselves that will be, in the end, of any value.

> Leading lights from cultural and political circles in the big cities have also been stranded on this barren stretch of heath . . . With one mighty convulsion all their scenery has collapsed about them, and now they stand around a little hesitantly and awkwardly on this drafty, open stage called Westerbork. These figures wrenched from their context still carry with them the restless atmosphere of a society more complicated than the one we have here.
>
> They walk along the thin, barbed-wire fence. Their silhouettes move, life-size and exposed, across the great stretch of sky. You cannot imagine it . . .
>
> Their armour of position, esteem, and property has collapsed, and now they stand in the last shreds of their humanity. They exist in an empty space, bounded by earth and sky, which they must fill with whatever they can find within them – there is nothing else. . . .
>
> Yes, it is true, our ultimate human values are being put to the test.

This remarkable letter says as much about Etty as it does about Westerbork. It tells of her journey, not least her sense of her journey as a Jew. It breathes her values; it speaks of her compassion; it reveals her capacity to see; and it echoes with her contemplative spirit. And, it contains no bitterness or hatred.

No doubt culled from her diaries, it was written in the winter of 1942 when she was back in Amsterdam. She eventually returned to Westerbork on 6th June 1943, and her long three-month stay there began.

## The hospital barracks

Soon after her arrival her need to care was given ample rein. She was given free access to the hospital barracks. She writes to her friend Maria: 'My soul is content Maria; I was given four hospital barracks today, one large and three small . . . The wonderful thing about it is that I now have free access to the whole complex of hospital barracks . . .'[4]

In his memoirs, Friedrich Weinreb gives us a glimpse of her doing her rounds:

> Etty Hillesum was a particularly welcome visitor. She did not come during visiting hours, but in connection with her job on the Jewish Council. Then she would walk round and ask if there were anyone who wanted to send a telegram via the Jewish Council. . . .
>
> (She) would walk round the beds with a leather bag over her shoulder, bending down towards every sick person and asking: 'Can I do anything for you?'[5]

## 'I started to shout and they saw me'

And then on 20th and 21st June the camp was overwhelmed by a vast influx. Over these two days there was a huge round-up of Jews in Amsterdam and 5,524 were sent to Westerbork. Among them were Etty's parents and her brother Mischa. She describes their arrival in a letter to her friend Milli Ortmann:

> The jam-packed freight train drew into the camp this morning. I stood beside it in the rain. The cars were shut tight, but there were a few small openings here and there high up, where the planks had been broken. Through one of these I suddenly spotted Mother's hat and Father's glasses and Mischa's peaky face. I started to shout and they saw me.[6]

The sheer numbers of these new detainees swamp the place. It is a grim moment and Etty is shocked by the sight of her parents struggling amid the mayhem, and for a moment her equilibrium is threatened. That night she writes to her friend Christine who knew her parents well:

> ... what we have now is a complete catastrophe. During the last twenty-four hours the camp has been engulfed by successive tidal waves of Jews. I must tell you: I was shocked by Father and Mother today, and Mischa, too. Father is completely helpless and his collar has grown a lot too big for him over the last twenty-four hours and the grey stubble of his beard is pathetic. But he waved a small Bible about this morning while we waited for hours and hours in the rain and found a marvellous quotation from Joshua. They are in a big barracks now, a jam-packed human warehouse: people sleeping three to a bed on narrow iron bunks, no mattresses for the men, nowhere at all to store anything, children terrified and screaming, the greatest possible wretchedness. I shall try to get through it as best I can, I even feel quite strong and brave, although sometimes I can see nothing but blackness and nothing makes any sense at all.[7]

## The mother figure

Now she is the mother figure, worrying about her family. Soon after their arrival she writes: 'I can see in myself the effects of worry about the family. It gnaws at you worse than anything else.'[8] She goes looking for them, drops in on them on her rounds, begs favours from her friend Christine – a pot of jam – for them. 'I wouldn't beg favours for myself,' she writes, 'but I would turn the world upside down to get my parents something to lighten their lives a little.'[9] She knows that although she herself is still 'exempt' from the transport, she will not be able to keep them off the lists for long, and anxiously wonders how they will cope and wishes –'above all else' – that she could spare them.[10]

## Overwhelmed by pity

Yet she questions whether the power of her 'pity' for them is in proportion, considering how much she has to care for others, and how
it may 'paralyze' her. In a letter to her housemates in Amsterdam she
says:

> There is a passage in the Bible from which I always draw new
> strength. I think it goes something like: 'He that loveth me, let
> him forsake his father and mother.' Last night I had to struggle
> again not to be overwhelmed by pity for my parents since it
> would paralyze me if I gave in to it. I know that we must not
> lose ourselves so completely in grief and concern for our fami-
> lies that we have little thought or love left for our neighbours.
> More and more I tend towards the idea that love for everyone
> who may cross your path, love for everyone made in God's
> image, must rise above love for blood relatives.[11]

It may not have been just her care for others that she feared would
be paralyzed if her 'pity' for her vulnerable parents and brother were
to overcome her. If she let her pity for them intrude too much into
her heart, her own capacity to survive would be at risk. It might open
her up to the terrible dangers of self-pity, and then she would be
swamped. On her last journey she decided she could not travel with
them in the same cattle wagon. She could cope with her own distress,
but not theirs as well.

But her blood ties ran deep – and in this time together at Westerbork were hugely positive. As she sees their courage she writes how
proud she is of them, and how much she has pleasure in them.
'Father and Mother give me a great deal of pleasure, for they are
coping in their own ways; I admire them tremendously.'[12] Her affection for them, for her father especially, surfaces again; she tells how
he teaches some boys who want to learn 'a little Greek and Latin', and
he goes 'through Homer, Ovid and Sallust' with them. 'For the rest,

he reads a great deal, philosophizes with ancient rabbis and old student friends, and now and then strolls with his daughter through the dusty sand of the hospital grounds.' And there is real warmth: 'We chuckle together a lot, Father and I; you can't really call it laughing. He has a primitive sense of humour, which becomes more profound and sparkling as the grotesque process of his reduction to poverty assumes ever more wretched dimensions.'[13]

After all the pain and anguish of her early life, her revulsion at her mother and her embarrassment about her father when he came and visited her at her house in Amsterdam, it is a moving picture of relationships renewed and transformed. A friend of Etty's, Philip Mechanicus, who also kept a diary in the camp, gives us a picture of the Hillesum family in their last days in Westerbork.

> Each day the wife kisses her husband, and the daughter kisses her father, full of tenderness, as a greeting and a farewell. Each day the daughter lovingly strokes her father's grey head, and in the lined face of her mother strokes smooth the wrinkles. Anxiously the sister watches her brother. A touching example of a happy family; an exemplary instance of mutual caring, of spiritual sharing, an inborn sense of the dignity of life. This family is caught up in the tornado of anti-Semitism, is on the brink of destruction. The shadow of the hopelessness that lies ahead already dims the mother's eyes, although in apparent calm she prepares for her unknown destination.[14]

## How did others see her?

As Etty visits in the hospital barracks, gives what support she can to those going on transport, and cares for the old, the sick and the despairing, we gain glimpses of how others see her. She was clearly a person who shone.

On 26th June in a letter back to her household she writes: 'Just now a woman who cleans for Kormann said to me: "You always look so radiant'."[15] Kormann himself – after their very first conversation back in July 1942 – told her: 'You are definitely no Dutchwoman; you have too much warmth.'[16] Writing to Christine van Nooten on 1st July, she comments: 'Yesterday the man who regularly cuts Father's hair said to me, "You're the sort of person who makes something of her life in any circumstances".'[17] And in early August, in a letter to Maria Tuinzing, she tells of the effects of a rainbow:

> Maria, dear friend, This morning there was a rainbow over the camp, and the sun shone in the mud puddles. When I went into the hospital barracks, some of the women called out, 'Have you got good news? You look so cheerful.' I considered saying something about Victor Emmanuel, about a popular government, and about peace being on the way. I couldn't fob them off with the rainbow, could I? – even though that was the only reason for my cheerfulness.[18]

## But what of her inner life?

To those around her, Etty brought comfort, warmth and vitality. She was a luminous person in a very bleak world. But what of herself over this period? What of her inner struggle to survive and stay sane amid such misery? To constantly be giving out to others is not sustainable without times of withdrawal and silence, retreat and solitude. In Amsterdam her room and desk had been her oasis – or the bathroom where she learnt to kneel on the coconut matting. But these were now only memories. How, in this crowded, chaotic hell, did she nourish her inner life?

It is hard to know. The diary she kept over this time is lost and her letters are public documents shared among friends. But she gives us glimpses.

First, through her friendships. She tells of how, when the pressures become intolerable, she goes for walks with Philip Mechanicus 'along the narrow, barren strip of earth between the ditch and the barbed wire'.[19] Jopie Vleeschhouwer, a fellow member of the Jewish Council, whom Etty refers to as her 'comrade-in-arms', is a special friend. With him she finds brief moments of space away from the tensions.

> This afternoon Jopie, who feels thoroughly sick and all in, stood together with his sister-in-arms Etty for at least a quarter of an hour looking up at one of these black and silver birds as it moved among the massive deep-blue rain clouds. We suddenly felt a lot less oppressed.[20]

Second, there is her love of nature and flowers. She writes of the wide sky and the sunsets, of the wild lupins in their colourful pro-fusion and the sea of heather, the rainbow, the clouds, and the wheeling birds.

And third, her prayer life. There is one letter in these last weeks where we gain a fuller insight into her inner life. On 18th August she wrote to her friend Henny Tideman who was also close to Spier, and whose simple faith had encouraged her. She tells Henny about resting on her bunk and writing her diary – and praying. And she sends Henny her prayer. It is, extraordinarily, very largely an outpouring of gratitude. God is the source and name of the gift of Life which still pulses through her and which she sees everywhere, even in this camp, and she finds herself overwhelmed with gratitude.

> My life has become an uninterrupted dialogue with You, oh God, one great dialogue. Sometimes when I stand in some corner of the camp, my feet planted on Your earth, my eyes raised towards Your heaven, tears sometimes run down my face, tears of deep emotion and gratitude.[21]

There is something very Jewish about the picture of this young woman, now standing erect among her people in this place of bitter exile, her feet on the earth and her eyes raised to heaven. But there is no lamentation or complaint. Astonishingly, she is simply grateful for the beauty and gift of life, which is so much greater than all this horror.

## Listening

Her eyes are raised to heaven. But her awareness of God remained focused within. She writes about how things come and go in inner rhythms, and always the need to listen. 'I have been terribly tired for several days, but that too will pass. Things come and go in a deeper rhythm, and people must be taught to listen; it is the most important thing we have to learn in this life.' And then it is as though Henny is forgotten, for the letter turns into her prayer as she speaks directly to God: 'I am not challenging You, oh God; my life is one great dialogue with You.' Her longing to be a writer is still there, but now she finds that all her attempts at words are eclipsed by the intensity of her devotion.

> I may never become the great artist I would really like to be, but I am already secure in You, God. Sometimes I try my hand at turning out small profundities and uncertain short stories, but I always end up with just one single word: God. And that says everything and there is no need for anything more. And all my creative powers are translated into inner dialogues with You.

The prayer somehow deeply settles her for she continues: 'The beat of my heart has grown deeper, more active, and yet more peaceful, and it is as if I were all the time storing up inner riches.'

The letter draws to an end with a reference to 'Jul' (Spier) whom both she and Henny had loved, and she tells her that 'there are many miracles in a human life. My own is one long sequence of inner miracles, and it's good to be able to say so again to somebody.'

One senses her loneliness, that she misses the friendships and discussions about the intimacies of faith. Perhaps she particularly misses the women who were close to her in Amsterdam. And perhaps she is particularly aware that this may be her last letter to Henny.

She ends with affection, telling her that her picture, tucked inside her copy of Rilke's *Book of Hours* lies under her pillow, next to Jul's photograph, and her small Bible.

And there is a PS: 'These few lines for Maria too, please, but nobody else. Bye.'

This powerful, sad and intimate letter reveals that beneath the chaos of this camp and the struggle to survive, the 'basic tune' of her heart still played on.

This was written in August. Not long before that, her life had become a lot less secure.

## 'An end will soon come to all the scribbling'

On 1st July she had written to Christine van Nooten: 'an end will come soon enough to all the scribbling.' She was referring to the fact that her privileged status as a member of the Jewish Council was about to end and she would become an internee. Sixty of the 120 people who worked for the Council had to go to back to Amsterdam. She was thankful that she was among those who stayed, not least because of her parents. The hope was that because of Mischa's exceptional musical talent, he, together with her parents, could be transferred to Barneveld, a castle in the province of Gelderland where a small number of exceptionally gifted Jews were held, exempt from deportation. She tells Christine,

> Luckily I am not one of the sixty, so I can keep protecting my parents as best I can . . . In Amsterdam the fight for Barneveld continues. I hope and pray that it will work out. I myself would ten times rather go to Poland or wherever, if only I am able to get my dear ones away from this place first.[22]

But the efforts of friends in Amsterdam were in vain, and the pressure grew. Each week the chances of them staying off the transport were slimmer. On Sunday 4th July she heard that they were on the list for the following Tuesday. Immediately she went to the authorities, desperately trying to get their names removed. This time she was successful, but she heard they must be ready for the next week. In distress she wrote to Milli Ortmann, who had tried so hard for the Barneveld option. She tells her that her strength had failed 'for the first time', and she had 'fainted right in the middle of the big barracks'.

> This morning yet another transport of 2,500 left. I managed with difficulty to keep my parents off it, but things are getting quite desperate. Good friends who have what is called influence told me this morning that my parents must make ready for next week's transport. The camp is being sucked dry. Everything is coming more and more to a head . . .[23]

Four days later she writes to Maria, realizing that once again she must accept what cannot be avoided. 'It will be my parents' turn to leave soon, if by some miracle not this week, then certainly one of the next. And I must learn to accept this as well.'[24]

Her own position was that all stamps (she had a red stamp in her papers declaring that she was 'exempt') had been declared invalid; it meant that she could now be sent on transport herself.

## The dread of the train

The life of the whole camp was governed by the dread of this train and the question of whose names were on the list. Westerbork existed to feed this train which was steadily devouring them – it had to be filled with its weekly quota of Jews. The camp commandant was finally responsible for seeing that the numbers were delivered, but the drawing up of the lists was left to the Jews themselves. Etty writes of a dark 'underworld' of power and influence, as to who goes and who does not. With the Jews conniving in their own destruction she feels ashamed of her own small part in it.

Tonight I shall be helping to dress babies and to calm mothers – and that is all I can hope to do. I could almost curse myself for that. For we all know that we are yielding up our sick and defenceless brothers and sisters to hunger, heat, cold, exposure, and destruction, and yet we dress them and escort them to the bare cattle cars – and if they can't walk we carry them on stretchers. What is going on, what mysteries are these, in what sort of fatal mechanism have we become enmeshed?[25]

## Seeing

In her descriptions of these trains – particularly in the second of the letters published in 1943 – Etty achieves the height of her powers as a writer and makes her most powerful contribution to the literature of the Holocaust. And in the telling of the story of the trains she reveals her greatest achievement: despite all that she has been through, she has not become hardened. Amid all that could so easily deaden the spirit, she remains alive. She is shaken to the core by what she sees, but is not numbed. She remains a reflective, feeling human being – 'the thinking heart of the barracks' – able to *see*.[26]

On the morning of 24th August, she sneaks into a barracks opposite where the train is being loaded to depart. She begins this long letter – what follows is but a brief summary – with words which prepare the reader for what is to come: 'There was a moment when I felt in all seriousness that after this night, it would be a sin ever to laugh again.'[27]

The letter focuses mostly on the victims, but at the beginning she tries to look at the perpetrators. From behind her glass protection she gazes intently at their faces:

When I think of the faces of that squad of armed, green-uniformed guards – my God, those faces! I looked at them, each in turn, from behind the safety of a window, and I have never been so frightened of anything in my life. I sank to my knees with the words that preside over human life: And God made man after His likeness. That passage spent a difficult morning with me.

'. . . no words and images are adequate', she writes, 'to describe nights like these'. But in a series of deft word sketches she struggles to capture what is unbelievable as she walks through the barracks in the hours before the transport leaves: 'I have to put it all down quickly, in a muddle, because if I leave it until later I probably won't be able to believe that it really happened.'

The babies are 'easily the worst' . . . 'those tiny piercing screams of the babies, dragged from their cots in the middle of the night to be carried off to a distant land'. And then in the hospital barracks she finds a young paralyzed girl who has just been learning to walk again.

'Have you heard? I have to go.' We look at each other for a long moment. It is as if her face has disappeared; she is all eyes. Then she says in a level, grey little voice, 'Such a pity, isn't it? That everything you have learned in life goes for nothing.' And, 'How hard it is to die.'

She catches sight of 'the ash-grey, freckled face of a colleague. She is squatting beside the bed of a dying woman who has swallowed some poison and who happens to be her mother . . .'

She tells of how 'the wailing of the babies grows louder still, filling every nook and cranny of the barracks, now bathed in ghostly light. It is almost too much to bear. A name occurs to me: Herod.'

She passes again the bed of the paralyzed girl:

I never saw such great big eyes in such a little face. 'I can't take it all in', she whispers to me. A few steps away stands my little hunchbacked Russian woman . . . as if spun in a web of sorrow. The paralyzed girl is a friend of her. Later she said sadly to me, 'She doesn't even have a plate; I wanted to give her mine, but she wouldn't take it.'

She comes across a young woman who is 'a recent arrival', and who is clearly 'used to luxury'.

> She has put on many different sets of underwear and other clothing all on top of one another . . . Now she looks lumpy and ridiculous. Her face is blotchy. She stares at everyone with a veiled, tentative gaze, like some defenceless and abandoned young animal. What will this young woman, already in a state of collapse, look like after three days in an overcrowded freight car with men, women, children, and babies all thrown together, bags and baggage, a bucket in the middle their only convenience?

She makes her way into other barracks. 'I see a dying old man being carried away, reciting the Shema to himself . . . I see a father, ready to depart, blessing his wife and child and being blessed in turn by an old rabbi with a snow-white beard . . .'

And then she turns her gaze back to the train and the guards 'swarming over the asphalt . . . guns over their shoulders'. Again she looks carefully, searching their faces for signs of humanity. 'I study their faces. I try to look at them without prejudice . . . Now I am transfixed with terror. Oafish jeering faces, in which one seeks in vain for even the slightest trace of human warmth.'

As her description continues, not a detail is missed. The women holding babies, the man from the camp Appeals Department who tries even at the last minute to get people off, 'a bent little old woman with a black old-fashioned hat' barring his way, 'gesticulating and brandishing a bundle of papers under his nose . . .'

And then the commandant appears. 'He now walks along the train with military precision.' Again she searches his face:

> It is a face that I am quite unable to read. Sometimes it seems to me to be like a long, thin scar in which grimness mingles with joylessness and hypocrisy. And there is something else about

him, halfway between a dapper hairdresser's assistant and a stagedoor Johnny . . . With military step he walks along the line of freight cars, bulging now with people. He is inspecting his troops: the sick, infants in arms, young mothers, and shaven-headed men. A few more ailing people are being brought up on stretchers. He makes an impatient gesture; they're taking too long about it.

She goes on to describe his Jewish secretary walking behind him, with 'fawn riding breeches', and 'the bully-boy figure' of the German Jew who makes the final decisions about the lists with his 'black top boots, black cap, black army coat with yellow star', parading beside him along the train. And then the final shocking moment when the doors are shut:

> My God, are the doors really being shut now? Yes they are. Shut on the herded, densely packed mass of people inside . . . The commandant takes a bicycle and rides along the entire length of the train. Then he makes a brief gesture like royalty in an operetta. A little orderly comes flying up and deferentially relieves him of his bicycle. The train gives a piercing whistle. And 1,020 Jews leave Holland.

## A profound and contradictory affirmation

Two days before she first went to Westerbork, Etty had written in her diary: '. . . there must be someone to live through it all and bear witness to the fact that God lived, even in these times'.

Perhaps the most remarkable thing about Etty Hillesum was that what she experienced did not embitter or dull her heart. And, because that was where her faith came from, still she believed.

With her clear gaze she saw terrible things happen. She was very close to the most vulnerable. She witnessed immense suffering and cruelty, and she suffered herself. There were moments when, as she wrote in one letter: 'I can see nothing but blackness and nothing makes any sense at all.' But, as we read through the whole span of her letters, such moments are rare.

Through them all and right to the end, the deeper sound in her heart was not despair but, extraordinarily, a strange kind of joy which would not leave her. She insisted and went on showing by the person she was that, despite everything, life is beautiful and good. She could not help but express and bear witness to this power of life which she knew within her and which she saw around her. This was her 'basic tune' which went on playing, whatever happened.

There is one passage in which this is particularly clear. It comes in a letter to Jopie and Klaas Smelik. In the early part she describes to them something of the misery of the place and she gives a glimpse of the cruelty of the Nazis as she describes a group of prisoners passing through the camp, but it is a prelude, perhaps a necessary prelude to what she really wants to say.

> The misery here is really indescribable. People live in those big barracks like so many rats in a sewer . . . One night last week a transport of prisoners passed through here. Thin, waxen faces. I have never seen such fatigue as I did that night . . . Early in the morning they were crammed into empty freight cars. Then another long wait while the train was boarded up. And then three days travel eastwards. Paper 'mattresses' on the floor for the sick. For the rest, bare boards with a bucket in the middle and roughly seventy to a sealed car . . . How many I wondered would reach their destination alive? And my parents are preparing themselves for just such a journey . . .'[28]

The letter continues talking about her father and joking with him about Westerbork being like a desert and Jews in the desert, and then eventually she comes to what she really wants to say. All this suffering and misery is not the final thing. She goes on to make a profound, astonishing and contradictory affirmation.

But I am digressing. All I wanted to say is this: The misery here is quite terrible; and yet, late at night when the day has slunk away into the depths behind me, I often walk with a spring in my step along the barbed wire. And then, time and again, it soars straight from my heart – I can't help it, that's just the way it is, like some elementary force – the feeling that life is glorious and magnificent, and that one day we shall be building a whole new world.

As we read this we may be amazed, and even question it, asking, how in such circumstances is this possible? How could it be possible to say such things, to feel such things? Is this real? Is it even, we may wonder, true?

And yet the testimony of the kind of person that she so clearly was – the testimony of the care and compassion which she so demonstrably showed to others; the testimony of those who met her and knew her, and spoke and wrote about her in the camp; and the power of her own words and the shape and texture of the long journey she has travelled – all these things bear witness that it was most deeply true.

On her long journey towards the camp, and in her life in the camp, Etty Hillesum found within herself an indestructible source of life and goodness and beauty that was greater and deeper and more enduring than all the terrible death and hatred which surrounded her, and which was eventually to engulf her.

## Marked by suffering

Her final long letter was to her friend Maria Tuinzing. The letter is dated 2nd September 1943. She had been in the camp for three months.

Although she says she is 'fine', the letter conveys a deep sense of sadness and exhaustion. She tells Maria of the priorities of each day, her Russian, her reading of the Psalms, her listening to people, and her search for some inner solitude.

Really I live here just as I used to with you in Amsterdam: in a community, but also very much for myself. This is possible even when one lives with other people, on them, under them, over them, in the middle of them.[29]

And then, after she has arranged a telegram code so that she can immediately get the message out if her parents have to go on transport, she comes to the heart of the letter.

She speaks of her weariness, how the place has aged her, but also, still, her faith in the goodness of life, and of the need to go on making sure that God is not lost. Perhaps she senses that it will not be long now, for she addresses her friend by name, uses it three times, as though she wants somehow to reach across the miles to her and give her some final message:

> How terribly young we were only a year ago on this heath, Maria! Now we've grown a little older. We hardly realise it ourselves: we have become marked by suffering for a whole lifetime. And yet life in its unfathomable depths is so wonderfully good, Maria – I have come back to that time and again. And if we just care enough, God is in safe hands with us despite everything, Maria.

Five days later, with her parents and her brother Mischa, she went on the train.

In the end it happened very suddenly. Late on Monday 6th September, an order came from The Hague that Mischa Hillesum and his family were to be sent on transport. Precisely what lay behind this order is hard to tell, but it appears to be because of a letter written by Etty's mother to Rauter who was Head of the German Police and the SS in the Netherlands, concerning Mischa, in the hope that he, and they, may be transferred. Whatever the hope behind this letter may have been, for a Jewess to write to Rauter – a convinced Jew hater and confidant of Himmler – was disastrous.

Gemmeker, the camp commandant, interpreted the order to mean that the entire family must go. For the parents, the situation was not such a surprise. They had been expecting it for many weeks and it was certainly going to happen anyway the following week. And if they went, it had always been clear that Mischa would go with them.

But for Etty it was a terrible and sudden surprise. Her friend Jopie Vleeschhouwer, writing afterwards to Amsterdam, says it did 'strike her down', though 'within the hour . . . she had recovered'.[30] And there was the difficulty that although she knew she would have to go at some point, she did not want to go with her parents, and preferred to go alone.

Immediately clothing and food and other items for the journey began to be gathered together. While Etty helped her parents, her girl friends packed her bag down to the smallest detail. Other friends made desperate efforts on her behalf to get her taken off the list, discussing with the camp officials and writing a letter as a last resort to the German Jew, Kurt Schlesinger, who was responsible for the names on the list. But it was to no avail. The commandant was implacable.

Jopie described her departure as she walked to the train:

Talking gaily, smiling, a kind word for everyone she met on the way, full of sparkling good humour, perhaps just a touch of sadness, but every inch the Etty you all know so well . . . I saw Mother, Father H, and Mischa get into Wagon No. 1. Etty finished up in No. 12 . . . Then a shrill whistle, the train started to move and the 1,000 'transport cases' were off. Another swift glimpse of Mischa waving hard through a chink in Wagon No. 1, then a cheerful 'Byyyeee' from Etty in 12, and . . . they were gone.[31]

Before the train left the Netherlands, Etty wrote a card to Christine van Nooten which she threw out through a crack in the boarded-up train. It was picked up and sent on by farmers. It read:[32]

Christine, opening the Bible at random, I find this: 'The Lord is my high tower.' I am sitting on my rucksack in the middle of a full freight car. Father, Mother, and Mischa are a few cars away. In the end, the departure came without warning. On sudden special orders from the Hague. We left the camp singing, Father and Mother firmly and calmly, Mischa too. We shall be travelling for three days. Thank you for all your kindness and care. Friends left behind will still be writing to Amsterdam; perhaps you will hear something from them. Or from my last long letter from camp.

Good-bye for now from the four of us.

Etty.

They arrived in Auschwitz on 10th September. She died there on 30th November.

Sculpture in memory of Etty Hillesum at Deventer
*Patrick Woodhouse*

Lupins and Watchtower at Westerbork today
*Patrick Woodhouse*

# Chapter 6

# A Woman for Our Time

*Somewhere deep inside me is a workshop in which Titans are forging a new world.*

In the town of Deventer in central Holland where she grew up, on the bank of the River IJssel, there stands a piece of sculpture in memory of Etty Hillesum. It consists of a very large block of stone – one edge of which is low and near the ground, suggesting the beginning of her life – which gently slopes upwards. Right through the middle of this huge piece there runs a jagged chasm which entirely splits it in two from top to bottom. The whole piece is a vivid memorial to a life of unusual strength and vitality which was violently 'interrupted'.

As you stand gazing at this stone in this place that Etty knew well, with the broad river sweeping past and the wide expanse of the Dutch landscape beyond, what strikes you is the insistence within the sculpture that her death, represented by the jagged chasm down the middle, was only an 'interruption'. On the other side of the 'interruption' of death, the stone continues and the second piece on the other side of the chasm is as vast as the first. This work of art is saying that though her life came to a violent end in Auschwitz, nevertheless it continues. The meaning and power of it flows on into our own time. It was not ended, merely 'interrupted'.

However, there is a distinct gap between the two pieces of rock, suggesting that for a time there was silence. Her voice did not speak. And that was indeed the case for a long time.

For 40 years her story remained almost entirely unknown. The only part of her writing that was known were the two long letters, first published clandestinely in 1943, which described Westerbork. Otherwise, together with millions of others, her life was consumed in the Holocaust. Except in the minds and hearts of those who had loved and admired her, and who had shared some small part of that life, she was lost for ever.

It was not until 1983, 40 years later, when an edited version of the diary, *An Interrupted Life* was published in English, that the world first came to hear of her. This book made her name known.

But for the English-speaking world it was not until nearly 20 years beyond that, in 2002, at the beginning of this new century, that it became possible to know her story in its completeness, for it was in that year that the complete and unabridged collection of the diaries and letters was published in English (the Dutch edition of the complete texts was first published in 1986).

It may be strangely appropriate that it has taken so long for her voice to be fully heard, for the story of her life challenges our context particularly. She has much to say to the issues of our time. This emotionally confused, sexually adventurous and intellectual young woman from a dysfunctional family, who was not interested in institutional religion, is a curiously modern person.

As we reflect on her more than 60 years after her death and hear her voice today, we need to allow her to sharply interrupt our lives, and we need to listen carefully as she invites us to find a truer and a deeper path.

There are four areas particularly in which she speaks.

First, she interrupts our scepticism about faith, and she invites us to believe again. Second, she interrupts our narrow assumptions about religion itself, and she invites us to pray. Third, she interrupts our easy hatreds of our enemy, and she invites us to see. Finally, she interrupts our despair about the future, and she invites us to be courageous.

## An invitation to believe again

Etty's story challenges the profound mood of scepticism which prevails in Britain and much of Western Europe, about whether faith in God can any longer be credible in the modern world, and she invites us to believe again.

Her diary and letters tell the story of an adventure of discovery. There is an entry in her diary when, impatient with the 'primitive' word 'God', she gives it a new definition and describes God as 'our greatest and most continuous inner adventure'.[1] The energy, dynamism and direction of this 'inner adventure' slowly but surely, like a great river, gathered up all that she was, and transformed her. Out of chaos there emerged emotional coherence; the power of her turbulent desire was transformed into a passion to care; a commitment to truth became a driving force; beneath her intellectual and emotional vitality she found an undercurrent of wisdom; and in the secrecy of an untidy bathroom her heart's deepest longing was met in the practice of adoration. Finally, even in the face of barbaric evil, she showed that a life can find within itself deep reservoirs of a strange joy. Above all, she bore witness to the reality of a deep *inner* dimension to the human person. It was to the inner spaciousness of her soul that she constantly returned, and it was this quality of depth which enabled her to face up to and deal with the barbarism and hatred around her.

Her life is a challenge to the radical doubt and scepticism of our time. Not the doubt of honest open-minded questioning which is an essential aspect of faith, but the kind of doubt which feeds cynical despair, because it blindly asserts that the adventure of faith is a delusion, and so doomed from the start.

This young woman took upon herself the extraordinary responsibility of making God credible, even in such a world as Westerbork. 'There must be someone to live through it all', she wrote, 'and bear witness to the fact that God lived, even in these times. And why should I not be that witness?'[2]

## Her way of faith

She fulfilled her task and was such a witness. And this witness invites us to explore her *way* of faith.

It was her practice of paying deep *attention* which transformed her. She first began to learn this on the brown coconut matting in the bathroom in the house in Amsterdam. The practice developed under the pressure of the terror until it became habitual. Through the months in the camp, as her contemplative heart attended to her inner life more and more, her direction was affirmed. She developed a deep sense of solidarity with her people, and she found she longed to care for the weakest and most vulnerable. Ever alert to signs of this life 'in all its thousands of nuances'[3] in the faces of those around her and in the natural world beyond the wire, she was determined not to be numbed by the cruelty but to go on *seeing*, so that she could tell the story of their fate. Increasingly she discovered that her practice of 'reposing in God'[4] released within her a deep wellspring of gratitude which at times was uncontainable. Even in the hell of this camp it would come flooding up from her depths. The picture of her standing in a corner of the camp, with tears of deep emotion and gratitude streaming down her face, is an image, an expression of profound mystical faith.

*Listening* was the primary mode of her believing. As her time in Westerbork passed, this practice deepened in intensity, although there were moments when 'nothing made sense'. In her letter to Henny Tideman she wrote: 'Things come and go in a deeper rhythm and people must be taught to listen; it is the most important thing we have to learn in this life.' And the listening led to a greater yielding – 'My life has become an uninterrupted dialogue with You Oh God'; and the yielding took her in only one direction: 'I always end up with just one single word: God.'

*This was her faith.* Did it sustain her to the end? Faith must cope with what attempts to block it off. Following the long letter of 24th August in which she described the oafish guards loading their pitiful human cargo, she wrote to Maria Tuinzing that she was 'strangely tired'. One senses that the outpourings of gratitude that she had written about just a few weeks before would now no longer be appropriate. Perhaps they were no longer possible. She had seen too much. 'Now we've grown a little older', she wrote. 'We hardly realise it ourselves: we have become marked by suffering for a whole lifetime.' But faith was not lost. '. . . life in its unfathomable depths is so wonderfully good Maria', she wrote. And God was not lost, 'if we just care enough, God is in safe hands with us, despite everything . . .'

Her faith did hold her to the end. She left the camp singing. Our last glimpse is of her sitting on her rucksack in the overcrowded boarded-up cattle car surrounded by scores of her fellow Jews with three days' journey ahead of them. On her final card that she sent to the outside world, the first thing that she wrote was a verse from the Psalms: 'The Lord is my high tower.'

It is hard to imagine a situation in which faith could be tested further. Her life speaks volumes for what faith is and what faith makes possible. She interrupts the scoffing scepticism of our time about religious faith, and she invites us too to learn what it means to listen deeply, and believe again.

## An invitation to pray

The second way in which Etty's life interrupts and challenges us is over our assumptions about religion itself – that institutions own and control it, about the question that lies at the heart of it, and how we think about its boundaries. Drawing on its diverse wisdoms, she invites us to find and explore our personal practice of faith.

Her journey to faith in God transformed her life, *but it happened outside any religious institution.* In this sense too, she is a contemporary figure.

Her story invites us to recognize journeys of faith that are outside the institutions of belief, and it encourages such journeying. It also challenges those who work within the institutions of religion to reflect more deeply on why it is they are so disregarded, and to listen to those beyond their borders.

Large numbers of people in the western world, particularly younger people, caught up in the pressures of a restless consumer society, find that its barren secularism offers them nothing in terms of the deeper questions of meaning. They can feel they are in a spiritual desert – and so, amid the demands and pressures and pace of lives lived at the surface of things, there is a deep hunger for 'spirituality'.

However, this interest in 'spirituality', which shows itself in all kinds of different ways, does not easily fit within the narratives and expectations of established religious institutions. So, in Britain and Europe (the situation in the United States appears to be different) there is the paradoxical situation that a growing interest in 'spirituality' corresponds with a decline in institutional churchgoing. This takes us to what lies at the heart of spirituality in a postmodern world.

In a helpful article entitled 'The Crisis of Postmodernity',[5] the writer and theologian Philip Sheldrake suggests that there is here a mismatch of questions. There is the question which the institutions of religion still largely focus on, namely 'What or who is God?' But, behind the 'contemporary spiritual quest' there is a different question (though, in the mystical tradition, a related one), namely, 'Who am I?' The problem for the religious institutions is that, in their creeds, liturgies and often in their preaching, they are exploring and expounding an answer to the former question, which increasingly is simply not being asked.

## The power of secularism

Secularism has done its powerful work in undermining the old worldview which traditional spiritualities took for granted and which placed the question of God at the centre of concern. Now, in the European world at least, the universal assumption is that the world, the universe, the human person and the course of history can only be properly understood in terms of the understandings of the disciplines of modern science. Quantum physics and cosmology will tell us about the nature of the universe; evolutionary biology will explain the world around us; biology, genetics, psychology and the study of the brain will unravel the nature of the human person; and the social, political and economic sciences will help us see and fathom the course of history.

This assumption has – with the exception of small pockets of fundamentalist thinking – become totally dominant in the post-Enlightenment western world and, in many people's minds, has undermined and rendered irrelevant and even absurd, the notion of God.

Etty would have understood this. There is one point in the diary when, after an intense discussion about faith, she goes home and asks herself: 'Isn't it all a lot of nonsense? Aren't they deluding themselves? That doubt always looms at the back of my mind?'[6]

## The question of the self

And so this question of God is no longer the point at which the contemporary spiritual quest begins. What drives that is the question – the bewildering, even mysterious question – of the *self*. Who am I, in the uniqueness of my feelings, relationships, reactions and sense of belonging or not belonging; in the very particular context of my life, my history and my possible future?

Religious institutions do not appear to have grasped the full force of this change: of the power of the secular earthquake in understanding which has occurred and which has shifted the focus of concern. They continue to behave as though the old worldview still held sway. They should not be so surprised that their numbers continue to decline.

Etty Hillesum speaks to the modern world because her journey began in psychotherapy, with the question so many others in various ways are asking: 'Who am I?' She began with the puzzling, disturbing enigma of *herself*, and her journey continued outside any religious institution.


## Five elements in her journey

There were five key elements in that journey: a relationship of unconditional acceptance within which she felt safe to explore her experience; intellectual exploration into the thought of some key writers, notably Jung and Rilke; the influence of her mentor, a person of faith, who introduced her to key religious texts, notably the Psalms, the New Testament and St Augustine, as well as several others; her own response to the urge she felt from within her, to pray; and the development of particular disciplines of the spiritual life.

Her particular pathway is a spur and encouragement to those who find belonging to the institutions of religion difficult. Whether or not a person remains a member of a church or synagogue or the institution of any other faith tradition, she invites us to go further in our *personal* exploration.

And her story invites us at some point to cross a boundary; to overcome what she experienced as a profound resistance.

The most intimate and perhaps important moment of her journey was when she first began to pray. She wrote that she suddenly 'found herself' kneeling on the brown coconut matting in the bathroom. It seemed to have happened involuntarily, in response to 'a great urge' from a deeper part of herself than her mind. She was deeply embarrassed by this and the 'critical rational atheistic bit' of her looked on in amazement and told her it was foolish. This is a key moment in the journey of faith: a moment when we need to let go of all our 'talking about', let go of the detachment of the questioning mind, and respond to some primal need of the heart, and – ignoring embarrassment and any sense of foolishness – dare to say 'Yes'.

Once this barrier is crossed – though the embarrassment will recur and the critical, rational part of us which is profoundly important will no doubt reassert itself – praying may, slowly, begin to become habitual, and even, as Etty found, deeply *necessary*. At one point in her diary she writes: 'I keep finding myself in prayer.'[7]

If we are to really enter into its potential – to discover where it may lead us – the disciplines of this life have to be *practised*. Like learning to paint, or play a musical instrument, it is hard work and cannot be learnt overnight. For Etty, her spirituality, her prayer, was about learning '*to live artistically*',[8] a phrase she took from Rilke. For this, she knew (echoing Rilke again) that 'patience is all'; patience and the practising of disciplines. And what are those disciplines?

- Silence – 'there is a vast silence in me that continues to grow'.[9]
- Solitude – 'deep inside us, all of us carry a vast and fruitful loneliness'.[10]
- Mindfulness, in being aware of, and dealing with, 'the wild herds' of thoughts and feelings.
- The use of images, learning both their power and their dangers.
- Reading the Psalms, taking just one phrase and planting it in the depths of the heart where its meaning can grow. And (for Etty most important of all).
- Learning to listen (to 'hearken') to 'everything reaching you from without ... and ... everything welling up from within'[11] – the development of an intuitive awareness of what is 'most essential and deepest' in ourselves, in others, in the inter-connectedness of life.

All this and more was part of her journey, which, particularly after she had left her friends in Amsterdam and Spier had died, was a solitary one. In her letter to Henny Tideman we glimpse her loneliness. For this work of spirituality to be sustained, we need friendships and communities. We also need, once we have sufficient confidence to cope with it, the wider challenge, help and corrective that the relevant religious institution can offer to our personal journey. Whatever our reservations, it is the bearer of our tradition: the place where our story is publicly held and celebrated. We belong to it – and we need to share in, and contribute to, its life.

And so, as well as offering encouragement to those outside religious institutions, Etty's story challenges those who have the responsibility of shaping such institutions, with a profound question. How can we ensure that our liturgies, rituals and ceremonies breathe with the sort of contemplative spirit which will attract those outside the institution as well as drawing in more deeply those who may be standing hesitantly on the edge?

## An inclusive ecumenical spirit

One way in which a contemplative spirit can be fostered is through reaching out to the traditions of other faiths. Etty had a wide and inclusive ecumenical spirit. In her quest she unself-consciously reached across boundaries into other faith traditions. Her example strikes chords with the modern seeker who will not be bothered from where wisdom comes (although the Church may well be). Etty interrupts our nervousness and says to us, *look wider.*

Those of us who belong to the Church have grown up within the boundaries of 'our' faith, as opposed to the faith of others – Jews, Muslims, Hindus, Buddhists, Sikhs. That is how we have been taught to think. There is a long and bloody history of fear and suspicion between the faith traditions of the world, of crusades and colonialism and inter-religious conflict. And this still continues, despite significant change and advances in dialogue and understanding in recent years. Nevertheless, still we tend to think only in terms of 'our' faith, and mentally we observe the boundaries. This is understandable, for each faith tradition has its own narratives and symbols, arising from its own particular history and context. Thus each faith tradition is different, and these differences need to be respected. But this approach can also be very limiting. We remain woefully ignorant of other faith traditions and we are still doubtful and timid about reaching across boundaries to learn from them.

Etty Hillesum was not concerned about any of this. The most fundamental theological idea for her lay at the root of the Jewish tradition: all human beings bear the Image of God within them, however buried and forgotten that image may be; all are created to grow into his likeness.

There are therefore no boundaries, and whatever can help in the digging out of this buried God from the heart is to be valued and cherished – it does not matter where it comes from. So, encouraged by Spier, Etty read the New Testament; she reached into the Gospels, especially Matthew, without any apparent self-consciousness that this is a 'different' tradition; she returned again and again to St Augustine – 'so austere and so fervent and so full of simple devotion in his love letters to God';[12] she kept quoting 'the Jew Paul' who had largely left behind his Jewish identity – but she is not bothered by that: it is his celebration of love in his letter to the Corinthians that worked on her 'like a divining rod'.[13] Her greatest love was for Rilke, who wrote the *Book of Hours* in the persona of a Russian Orthodox monk. When her little bag was searched on her arrival at Westerbork, there, lying side by side, were the Koran and the Talmud; and during her last year she read a lot of Meister Eckhart.[14]

Like the Cistercian monk Thomas Merton, who welcomed and embraced insights from Zen Buddhism and the Sufi tradition, Etty calls us to realize that insights from different faith traditions meet and complement one another in the depths of the heart of the contemplative where there is adoration of the One who is beyond all names.

### An invitation to see

Third, Etty's story interrupts the easy way we talk of and envisage – or fail to 'envisage' (for this word suggests the seeing of a face) – our enemy. In our understanding of the primary conflict of our time, she invites us to bridge chasms of misunderstanding in our world and explore what may be involved in *seeing*, and so open the way to justice and reconciliation.

Her time was radically different from ours, but there is some similarity in at least the bare outline of our two very different contexts insofar as they focus on questions of hatred and attitudes to enemies.

As a Jew in Holland in 1941, Etty was faced with an enemy blinded by a terrible ideology of racial purity that was fired by hatred, and which aimed to destroy her race.

Today, the western world faces a terrorist enemy whose terrorism is driven by a deeply distorted religious ideology. This carries within it a deep hatred of the western world, particularly America. This hatred has led to terrible acts of violent destruction against the citizens of western countries. And in response this has aroused fear.

How Etty responded to her reality interrupts and questions the ways in which we may respond to ours.

First, she refused to hate her enemy. It is, simply in itself, a disturbing stance, for it means we have to think. To refuse to hate is, in the final analysis, to refuse to see someone, or a group of people – who manifestly *are* an enemy bent on your destruction – *as* an 'enemy'. It is to live with this paradox and involves – even as your country defends itself against their hatred – trying to pay attention to the wider and more complex context of their lives, and ask, searchingly, why are they, and why are we, caught up in such hatred? Who are we to them, and who are they to us?

## The enemy as a human being

Despite the clear understanding of what she faced, Etty struggled to see those who persecuted her, *as human beings*. She looked into the face of the 'pitiful' young Gestapo officer who threatened her at the registration desk, and she sought to connect with his humanity; she searched the faces of the oafish guards in the hope of detecting some faint flicker of life even in them. Just occasionally her looking was rewarded. Her friend Liesl tells of a German soldier whom she met in the street, who had pushed a note into her hand telling her she reminded him of a rabbi's daughter whom he, the German soldier, had nursed, and he would like to visit her. It was a small ray of light in the gloom of hatred. Etty wrote: 'Out of all those uniforms, one has been given a face now. There will be other faces, too, in which we shall be able to read something we understand . . .'[15] *A uniform which has been given a face.*

It was a wonderful exception. Amid the carnage of war, she kept looking for other faces. 'I try', she wrote, 'to look things straight in the face, even the worst crimes and discover the small naked human being amid the monstrous wreckage caused by man's senseless deeds.'[16]

Amid the monstrous wreckage of the atrocities we have experienced – the terrible 'senseless deeds' that have shaped the events of this new century – it is very hard for us to see the perpetrators of those deeds as 'small', 'naked' – i.e. vulnerable, and 'human'. But in all conflicts and attacks that is always the deepest reality which must be searched for. Hidden behind the distorted face of those who do such monstrous deeds, there is somewhere *a small vulnerable human being.* Evil, she knew, is in the end only a mask, a gross distortion which can entirely obscure the true face of the person underneath, *but nevertheless still, only a mask.* 'No one', she insisted to Klaas, 'is really "bad" deep down.' On the day she could not see a face on the commandant who was sending a thousand Jews to their deaths, but only 'a long thin scar', she did not surrender that conviction. She never gave up in the hope of seeing – across the chasms of war – the face of the other who is human too. Like us, they too, are bearers of the Divine image however deeply marred and buried it may be, and so they are people to whom we belong.

To remove from the mind the label of 'enemy' is like removing the blinds from a window and letting the light in. If you will not hate them, then you may begin to see them. Those who wish to destroy you are human beings. They have stories to tell, and families and communities from which they come, as we have. They have been shaped, as we have, by their very particular personal and social contexts. Their loyalties, customs and traditions make them who they are. And they have sorrows and injustices and humiliations to cope with also – sometimes terrible injustices and humiliations.

This taking down of the blinds enabled Etty in her time to see war as human-sized, and so to de-construct its mythology.

Though stubbornly person-centred, she also recognized that wars and conflicts are bigger than individuals. People get drawn into systems which take them over: '. . . you cannot take your hate out on individuals', she wrote, 'no one person is to blame, the system has taken over . . .' By this she meant the Nazi ideology which had poisoned the collective mind of an entire people '. . . an ominous structure capable of crashing down on top of all of us, on top of the interrogators as well as on the interrogated'.[17]

This phenomenon too she invites us to see and understand: to deconstruct collective systems of thought – including our own – and ask how and why they have come about, and what lies behind them. People on both sides of conflicts can become blind. All this is only possible if there is no hatred, for only then can we be sufficiently dispassionate to have some chance of seeing.

When the Germans invaded Holland and the persecution began, hatred became the currency of every conversation among the Jews, so they could not *see*, they could only hate. They could not 'grasp major trends', 'fathom underlying currents', they could not ask the question, 'Why?' And her friends didn't want to. They preferred the easy way. They kept the blinds up and just talked of hatred – everything 'clear-cut and ugly'.

As one realizes the intensity of her passion to unveil truth, the reader of the New Testament is reminded of the words that are repeated again and again like a gentle, insistent invitation to the reader at the beginning of the Gospel of John: 'Come . . . and *see*'.

## An invitation to be courageous

Finally, Etty interrupts the mood of our time and invites us to be courageous.

Courage was perhaps her greatest virtue. With courage she faced up to her personal chaos and found her self; with courage she went deeper in her journey of exploration and discovered the divine ground of her heart; with courage she refused to hate; and with courage she refused to hide, choosing to embrace the fate of her people and to lose her life. She shows that a truly human life is lived on the courageous and paradoxical path of self-discovery and self-emptying. So in the midst of darkness she found joy, and was alive in that place in spite of the power of death.

In the circumstances of our time, particularly amid our fear and pessimism about the future, she invites us, too, to live courageously.

Those who lived through the decade of the 1960s will look back – no doubt with a heavy dose of nostalgia – and remember it as a time of great optimism, liberation and experiment; a time of breaking out of the dull straitjacket of all that had inhibited life through the austerity of the post-war years. The 1960s invited exploration of a new future. With its colour and excess, its pushing against all boundaries, it was a decade that generated a feeling that change was in the air and anything was possible.

Forty years later, as we reach the end of the first decade of the twenty-first century, we are in a very different place. That mood of optimism has entirely evaporated and given way to a deep sense of pessimism as to what the future holds. It is not too much to say that many people, perhaps older people particularly, feel – in the words of Etty Hillesum – that the world 'is in a state of collapse'. Not the violent, apocalyptic collapse that she lived through, but *a slow and steady disintegration of confidence about the future.*

This pessimism becomes focused on different concerns. Climate change, with all its huge and frightening ramifications, is the most obvious, but there are others: for example, the possible proliferation of nuclear weapons, or the huge question of the sustainability, in terms of food and resources, of a world population projected to rise from over six and a half billion now, to nine billion by 2050. All these can seem insuperably daunting issues, both for ourselves and for future generations. At a domestic level in Britain, pessimism tends to focus on symptoms of deep social malaise in what appears to be an increasingly fragmented and aimless society.

Speaking out of a world that was violently disintegrating around her, Etty interrupts our pessimism and invites us to be courageous.

She invites us to look whatever difficult situations we may face straight in the eye, whether they are personal or much wider, and to engage with them, seeking *life* through that engagement.

## Integrating the negative

In her case this engagement involved the clear-eyed acceptance of what could not be avoided, a steadfast refusal to indulge in illusion, and the conscious bearing of sorrow and loss. She faced up to a situation that seemed entirely hopeless, and integrated into herself what seemed utterly negative, and it released her to face the present with courage, and to believe in the future with hope. This was her transformation. It was, as we have seen, a battle – she writes of it as 'a struggle' – but through such honesty and courage she was no longer a victim of her situation but became fully *herself*, within it. At the beginning of July 1942 she wrote:

> Yes, we carry everything within us, God and Heaven and Hell and Earth and Life and Death and all of history. The externals are simply so many props; everything we need is within us. And we have to take everything that comes: the bad with the good which does not mean we cannot devote our life to curing the bad.[18]

It is an extraordinarily inclusive statement. Etty claims that she carries 'God' and 'Heaven' within her, and perhaps by this she meant moments and memories of peace (in the sunshine outside by the chestnut tree?), or friendship (in her household?), or understanding (with Spier?), or community (the musical evenings they shared?). But she writes that she carries 'Hell' and 'Death' within her also: what did she mean with *these* words? Was it the immediate violence around her? Or perhaps the memory of friends who have suddenly disappeared? Or the sight of wrecked homes blasted to bits by bombs? Or the terror in the faces of children? Or the hunger and the fear among the vulnerable old people? Or was she referring to the future which they all faced: the suffering and death to come in an extermination camp, which she believed could not be avoided?

All of these things she saw, or struggled to absorb. She held it all *within her*. She would not shut out the reality of what was going on, nor turn her eyes away from what was to come. Everything must be 'carried' within. It was all part of her.

But to do this – fully to accept the negative, and to live with such undefended openness to the totality of what life throws at us – takes huge courage.

## The courage of despair

One writer who has explored this theme of courage perhaps more than any other in our time is the twentieth-century theologian Paul Tillich. In his book *The Courage to Be*, which is a study of the meaning of courage in the face of anxiety and despair as it is experienced in the modern period, he uses a phrase which seems deeply contradictory: '*The courage of despair*'.[19]

We may think of courage and despair as opposites, and assume that we have to choose one or the other, for they cannot live together. A person threatened by despair may determinedly walk forward into the future, refusing to acknowledge their despair in the fear that, if they do, they will be undone. All is well and all shall be well. This is their courage. They may for a time win out over their despair, but they will remain a brittle person, haunted by the fear that the despair may return, for it will not have gone far away. Or alternatively a person may surrender to despair and become overwhelmed by it, and curl up in a corner and wish to die, feeling that nothing can be changed and all is hopeless.

It would seem that the choice is either courage *or* despair. But what does it mean to put these words together and speak of 'the courage *of* despair'?

This gives courage an altogether deeper meaning. It is 'the courage to be' *in spite of* death, fate, meaninglessness or despair. It is about affirming life in the face of what seems unalterable in your situation. You do not pretend that despair is not there. You acknowledge it: it is part of you. *But, by living courageously in the face of it, you rob it of its power.* This is the courage of despair. To live with this kind of courage is immensely challenging. It is the challenge of becoming an integrated and fully human person; and, as we shall see, it is about more even than integration.

Remarkably, in one of her letters from Westerbork, we find that Etty Hillesum uses this expression herself. The letter, which has only recently come to light and is in the Dutch (but not the English) edition of the diaries and letters, is dated 24th August 1942, and it begins with this striking phrase.[20] Written over several days to a friend in Amsterdam, Hes Hymans, it is an account of daily life in the camp. On the face of it, the letter contains nothing that is particularly profound. There are no great moments of spiritual insight, no tears of deep emotion, no searing description of the train. But through it we see Etty in the ordinariness of her life, giving, in the face of the all-pervasive despair, gentle and attentive care to people. As she lives courageously in this camp, we begin to glimpse why she is described elsewhere as 'radiant' – why she shone. It was simply that, as she went round in that place where everyone was doomed to death, she affirmed and embodied life. She loved people and, against the utterly bleak backdrop of their existence, she offered warmth and care, humour and kindness. Even in the face of death, she would not be daunted.

She writes: 'With the courage of despair I shall try to steal from this day one hour to tell you a few trifles which even happen in the heath land of Drenthe.' She goes on to describe where she is sitting to write the letter – on a wooden bench with her back against wooden barracks and in front of her is the sight of waving blue heather. She writes that 'it is good to live even behind barbed wire and in draughty barracks if one lives with the necessary love for people and for life'. She tells of the greetings given to her from every side when she returned, which were 'unbelievably friendly, as if, after an absence of many years, I came back among good old friends'. (She had been away for a week in mid-August.) The letter describes the ordinary things that engage her attention: pouring out coffee, cutting and giving out bread, reading Meister Eckhart and scrubbing the toilets, walking round with dry biscuits and tea, listening and talking to a young girl who was nervous of sharing her poetry and encouraging her, 'and telling her of those things that are the most important in life', and speaking 'to many people'. She tells how she comforts a woman weeping on her right shoulder while a small child falls asleep on her left, and of the time she spends with 'very many old people. One was blind and one with a crinkly parchment-like face who was carried away on a stretcher.'

Amid this giving to others, the letter reveals her attentiveness to her own needs and those things which nourish her. She tells of taking refuge in her sleeping hut, for a 'person needs to be alone'; and she writes of eating red cabbage with friends and reading Rilke's poems from the *Book of Hours* aloud together, with one of them 'thundering' out – 'so that it sounded far over the lupin field to the de-lousing hut' – the last words of the poem: 'God, you are great'. As this friend reads Rilke aloud, she notices how he becomes 'progressively more youthful'. But the reading is constantly interrupted. 'More people come in', she writes, 'with many anxieties and questions and worries and we put Rilke aside again.'

Towards the end she writes, '. . . this afternoon more people will be coming, it just never stops any more', and then, playfully, and with a touch of sorrow – and here we gain just a glimpse of what she is holding within her – she rebukes the sun which has the audacity to go on shining over them in such a place: 'and the sun stands so openly beaming and shining above the heather that it should really be ashamed of itself'.

In this ordinary letter we see this young woman, gently and without any drama, caring, serving, listening, and – in this place of death – giving out life. Punctuated with gentle irony and humour, it is full of warmth and compassion. And there is no despair, except in the opening phrase. The despair is not denied: it exists, *but it is entirely swallowed up in courageous living.*

## A revealing of God

Paul Tillich writes that such courage – the courage to affirm life in the face of despair; to care and serve and give and smile upon others in such a situation – is more than a revealing of the life of an integrated person. It is a revealing of God: of the power of 'being-itself'.

'There are no valid arguments', he writes, 'for the "existence" of God, but there are acts of courage in which we affirm the power of being . . . Courage has revealing power, the courage to be is the key to being-itself.'[21]

Tillich, who was born, grew up and developed his teaching career as a philosopher and theologian in Germany, was deeply conscious of what the Holocaust meant. He left Germany because of the Nazis in 1933. In one of his sermons, published just two years before his death, he sums up what this kind of courage – so manifest in Etty's life – reveals: the power and triumph of love.

> It is love, human and divine, which overcomes death in nations and generations and in all the horror of our time . . . Death is given power over everything finite, especially in our period of history. But death is given no power over love. Love is stronger. It creates something new out of the destruction caused by death; it bears everything and overcomes everything. It is at work where the power of death is strongest, in war and persecution and homelessness and hunger and physical death itself. It is omnipresent and here and there, in the smallest and most

hidden ways as in the greatest and most visible ones, it rescues life from death. It reaches each of us, for love is stronger than death.[22]

On 13th October 1942, Etty Hillesum wrote the final sentence of the diary which has survived her. It reads:

'We should be willing to act as a balm for all wounds.'

# Some Significant Dates

| | |
|---|---|
| 15th January 1914 | Etty Hillesum is born in Middelburg, Holland |
| March 1932 | Etty leaves home to be a student in Amsterdam |
| March 1937 | Etty moves into the home of Han Wegerif |
| 15th May 1940 | Holland capitulates to the Germans |
| 3rd February 1941 | Etty meets Julius Spier |
| 8th March 1941 | Etty writes a letter to Julius Spier |
| 9th March 1941 | The first entry in the diary |
| 9th March 1941– 13th October 1942 | The total period of the diary (11 books, though number 7 is lost, and the diary kept during her time in Westerbork is lost) |
| 20th January 1942 | The Wannsee Conference meets to implement the 'Final Solution' |
| 1st July 1942 | The Germans take over Westerbork, which changes from a refugee camp to a transit camp |
| 3rd–29th July 1942 | The period of the tenth exercise book of the diary |
| 16th July 1942 | Etty begins work at the Jewish Council |
| 30th July 1942 | Etty goes to Westerbork to work in 'Social Welfare for People in Transit' |

| | |
|---|---|
| 14th–21st August 1942 | Etty is away from Westerbork in Amsterdam and Deventer |
| 21st August 1942 | Etty returns to Westerbork |
| 15th September 1942 | Spier dies; Etty is back in Amsterdam |
| 15th September–13th October 1942 | The period of the eleventh and last book of the diary |
| 15th September–20th November 1942 | Etty is in Amsterdam, increasingly unwell |
| 20th November–5th December 1942 | Etty is in Westerbork, but unwell |
| 5th December 1942–5th June 1943 | Etty returns to Amsterdam and remains there because of sickness |
| End of December 1942 | First of the two long letters about Westerbork – to 'two sisters in the Hague' – published illegally during the war |
| 6th June 1943 | Etty leaves Amsterdam for the last time and goes to Westerbork |
| 5th July 1943 | Etty becomes a camp internee (the end to special status of Jewish Council personnel at Westerbork) |
| 24th August 1943 | Second of the two long letters about Westerbork published during the war |
| 7th September 1943 | Etty, her parents and her brother are put on transport |
| 10th September 1943 | They arrive at Auschwitz |
| 30th November 1943 | Etty dies at Auschwitz |

# Notes

### Who Was Etty Hillesum?

1. *Etty: The Letters and Diaries of Etty Hillesum 1941–1943, Complete and Unabridged*, Klaas A. D. Smelik (ed.), Arnold J. Pomerans (trans.) (Eerdmans Publishing Company; Novalis, 2002), Introduction, p. xii.

### Chapter 1: An Emerging Self

1. *Etty: The Letters and Diaries of Etty Hillesum 1941–1943, Complete and Unabridged*, Klaas A. D. Smelik (ed.), Arnold J. Pomerans (trans.) (Eerdmans Publishing Company; Novalis, 2002), p. 3.
2. Ibid., p. 6.
3. Ibid., p. 198.
4. Ibid., p. 249.
5. Ibid., p. 168.
6. Ibid., p. 79.
7. Ibid., p. 83.
8. Ibid., pp. 87, 88.
9. Ibid., p. 80.
10. Ibid., p. 207.
11. Ibid., p. 159.
12. Ibid., p. 146.
13. Ibid., p. 141.
14. Ibid., p. 86.
15. Ibid., p. 146.
16. Ibid., p. 160.
17. Ibid., p. 341.
18. Ibid., pp. 198, 199.
19. Ibid., p. 7.
20. Ibid., p. 4.
21. Ibid., p. 278.
22. Ibid., p. 6.
23. Ibid., p. 735 (note from p. 427, 'Netty's diary').
24. Ibid., p. 6.
25. Ibid., p. 5.
26. Ibid., p. 55.
27. Ibid., p. 71.
28. Ibid., p. 58.
29. Ibid., p. 91.
30. Ibid., pp. 4, 6, 7.
31. Ibid., p. 8.
32. Ibid., p. 13.
33. Ibid., pp. 41, 42, 43.
34. Ibid., p. 13.
35. Ibid., p. 27.
36. Ibid., p. 33.
37. Ibid., p. 36.
38. Ibid., p. 48.
39. Ibid., quotations in this paragraph: pp. 54, 58, 68, 75, 92, 111, 120, 128, 141.
40. Ibid., p. 72.
41. Ibid., p. 62.
42. Ibid., p. 25.
43. Ibid., p. 313.
44. Ibid., p. 365.
45. Ibid., p. 212.
46. Ibid., p. 84.
47. Ibid., p. 162.
48. Ibid., p. 204.
49. Ibid., p. 207.
50. Ibid., p. 240.
51. Ibid., p. 89.

52. Ibid., p. 305.
53. Ibid., p. 210.
54. Ibid., p. 211.
55. Ibid., p. 558.
56. Ibid., p. 246.
57. Ibid., p. 531.
58. Ibid., p. 326.
59. Ibid., p. 516.

### Chapter 2: Discovering God

1. *Etty: The Letters and Diaries of Etty Hillesum 1941–1943, Complete and Unabridged*, Klaas A. D. Smelik (ed.), Arnold J. Pomerans (trans.) (Eerdmans Publishing Company; Novalis, 2002), p. 198.
2. Ibid., Introduction, p. xi.
3. Ibid., p. 51.
4. Ibid., p. 53.
5. Ibid., p. 53.
6. Ibid., pp. 25, 26.
7. Ibid., p. 42.
8. Ibid., p. 120.
9. Ibid., pp. 56, 57.
10. Ibid., p. 10.
11. Ibid., pp. 93, 94.
12. Ibid., p. 122.
13. Ibid., p. 126.
14. Ibid., p. 139.
15. Ibid., p. 68.
16. Ibid., p. 126.
17. Ibid., pp. 4, 6, 3, 42.
18. Ibid., p. 60.
19. Ibid., p. 435.
20. Ibid., pp. 60, 204.
21. Ibid., p. 209.
22. Ibid., p. 387.
23. Ibid., p. 181.
24. Ibid., p. 187.
25. Ibid., p. 83.
26. Thomas Merton, *Seeds of Contemplation* (Anthony Clarke Books, 1972; first published as *New Seeds of Contemplation*; Burns & Oates, 1962), p. 28.
27. *Etty*, op. cit., pp. 90, 91.
28. Ibid., p. 91.
29. Ibid., p. 103.
30. Ibid., p. 148.

31. Ibid., p. 165.
32. Ibid., p. 181.
33. Ibid., p. 194.
34. Ibid., p. 212.
35. Ibid., p. 216.
36. Ibid., p. 320.
37. Ibid., p. 458.
38. Ibid., p. 469.
39. Ibid., p. 497.
40. Ibid., p. 547.
41. Ibid., quotations in this paragraph: pp. 53, 175, 197, 223.
42. Ibid., p. 234.
43. Ibid., p. 246.
44. Ibid., p. 174.
45. Ibid., p. 426.
46. Ibid., p. 262.
47. Ibid., p. 228.
48. Ibid., p. 309.
49. Ibid., p. 532.
50. Ibid., p. 275.
51. Ibid., p. 364.
52. Ibid., p. 386.
53. Dietrich Bonhoeffer, *Letters and Papers from Prison* (Fontana, 1959; first published SCM Press, 1953), p. 122.
54. *Etty*, op. cit., p. 586.
55. Ibid., pp. 488, 489.
56. Ibid., p. 489.

### Chapter 3: Refusing to Hate

1. *Etty: The Letters and Diaries of Etty Hillesum 1941–1943, Complete and Unabridged*, Klaas A. D. Smelik (ed.), Arnold J. Pomerans (trans.) (Eerdmans Publishing Company; Novalis, 2002), p. 18.
2. Ibid., pp. 112, 113.
3. Ibid., p. 19.
4. Ibid., p. 21.
5. Ibid., p. 259.
6. Ibid., p. 20.
7. Ibid., pp. 258, 259.
8. Ibid., p. 384.
9. Ibid., p. 163.
10. Ibid., p. 19.
11. Laurens van der Post, *Jung and the Story of our Time* (Penguin, 1978;

first published Hogarth Press, 1976),
Prologue, p. x.
12. *Etty*, op. cit., p. 180.
13. Ibid., p. 159.
14. Ibid., p. 259.
15. Ibid., p. 181.
16. Ibid., pp. 528, 529.
17. Ibid., p. 245.
18. Ibid., p. 543.
19. Ibid., p. 496.
20. Ibid., p. 494.
21. Ibid., p. 252.
22. Ibid., p. 595.
23. Ibid., p. 500.
24. Ibid., p. 342.
25. Ibid., p. 325.
26. Ibid., p. 232.
27. Ibid., p. 325.
28. Ibid., p. 453.
29. Ibid., p. 422.
30. Ibid., p. 436.
31. Ibid., p. 349.
32. Richard Harries, *Art and the Beauty of God* (Continuum, 1993), p. 39.
33. *Etty*, op. cit., p. 500.
34. Ibid., p. 299.
35. Ibid., p. 300.
36. Ibid., p. 253.
37. Ibid., p. 252.
38. Ibid., p. 355.
39. Ibid., p. 491.
40. Ibid., p. 500.
41. Ibid., p. 308.
42. Ibid., p. 465.
43. Ibid., p. 586.
44. Ibid., p. 183.
45. Ibid., p. 182.
46. Ibid., p. 517.
47. Ibid., p. 590.

### Chapter 4: Losing Her Life

1. *Etty: The Letters and Diaries of Etty Hillesum 1941–1943, Complete and Unabridged*, Klaas A. D. Smelik (ed.), Arnold J. Pomerans (trans.) (Eerdmans Publishing Company; Novalis, 2002), p. 358.
2. Ian Kershaw, *Hitler, the Germans and the Final Solution* (Yale University Press, 2008), pp. 267, 268.
3. *Etty*, op. cit., p. 461.
4. Ibid., p. 463.
5. Ibid., p. 464.
6. Ibid., this and following three quotations, pp. 466, 467.
7. Ibid., p. 485.
8. Ibid., pp. 485, 486.
9. Ibid., p. 468.
10. Ibid., p. 488.
11. Ibid., pp. 479, 480.
12. Ibid., p. 483.
13. Ibid., p. 483.
14. Ibid., p. 484.
15. Ibid., p. 487.
16. Ibid., p. 519.
17. Ibid., p. 487.
18. Ibid., p. 761 (note from p. 594, 'kidnapped . . . people').
19. Ibid., p. 476.
20. Ibid., p. 475.
21. Ibid., p. 476.
22. Ibid., p. 476.
23. Ibid., p. 477.
24. Ibid., p. 469.
25. Ibid., p. 473.
26. Ibid., p. 503.
27. Ibid., p. 491.
28. Ibid., this and the following two quotations, p. 493.
29. Ibid., p. 494.
30. Ibid., p. 495.
31. Ibid., p. 491.
32. Ibid., p. 508.
33. Ibid., pp. 498, 499.
34. Ibid., p. 499.
35. Ibid., p. 508.
36. Ibid., p. 511.
37. Ibid., p. 531.
38. Ibid., pp. 516, 517.
39. Ibid., pp. 569, 570.
40. Ibid., p. 519.
41. Ibid., p. 520.
42. Ibid., p. 537.
43. Ibid., p. 510.
44. Ibid., p. 484.
45. Ibid., p. 506.

## Chapter 5: Seeing Differently

1. *Etty: The Letters and Diaries of Etty Hillesum 1941–1943, Complete and Unabridged*, Klaas A. D. Smelik (ed.), Arnold J. Pomerans (trans.) (Eerdmans Publishing Company; Novalis, 2002), p. 616.
2. Ibid., pp. 580–90, for all the quotations from this letter.
3. Ibid., p. 768 (note from p. 607, 'Weinreb').
4. Ibid., p. 603.
5. Ibid., p. 768 (note from p.607, 'Weinreb').
6. Ibid., p. 603.
7. Ibid., p. 604.
8. Ibid., p. 607.
9. Ibid., p. 614.
10. Ibid., p. 625.
11. Ibid., p. 641.
12. Ibid., p. 625.
13. Ibid., p. 633.
14. Ibid., p. 767.
15. Ibid., p. 607.
16. Ibid., p. 598.
17. Ibid., p. 613.
18. Ibid., p. 631 (note on page 776, 'Victor Emmanuel': On 25 July 1943 the Italian king Victor Emmanuel III (1869–1947) ordered the arrest of Mussolini, following the landing of the Allies on Sicily, 9 July 1943).
19. Ibid., p. 607.
20. Ibid., p. 621.
21. Ibid., p. 640, for all the quotations from this letter.
22. Ibid., p. 612.
23. Ibid., p. 623.
24. Ibid., p. 627.
25. Ibid., p. 645.
26. Ibid., p. 543.
27. Ibid., pp. 644–54, for all the quotations from this letter.
28. Ibid., p. 616, for this and the following quotation.
29. Ibid., p. 657, for this and the following quotation.
30. Ibid., p. 666.
31. Ibid., p. 668.
32. Ibid., p. 658.

## Chapter 6: A Woman for Our Time

1. *Etty: The Letters and Diaries of Etty Hillesum 1941–1943, Complete and Unabridged*, Klaas A. D. Smelik (ed.), Arnold J. Pomerans (trans.) (Eerdmans Publishing Company; Novalis, 2002), p. 439.
2. Ibid., p. 506.
3. Ibid., p. 584.
4. Ibid., p. 519.
5. Philip F. Sheldrake, 'The Crisis of Postmodernity'. *Christian Spirituality Bulletin*, Summer 1996, 6–9.
6. *Etty*, op. cit., p. 159.
7. Ibid., p. 484.
8. Ibid., p. 243, for this and the following quotation.
9. Ibid., p. 503.
10. Ibid., p. 305.
11. Ibid., p. 326.
12. Ibid., p. 546.
13. Ibid., p. 256.
14. Ibid., p. 771. Note for p. 613, 'In the final year of her life Etty read a great deal of Meister Eckhart's writings, according to a note made by Maria Tuinzing in Etty's copy of *Ein Brevarium aus seinen Schriften*' (Leipzig: Insel Verlag, s.d.).
15. Ibid., p. 465.
16. Ibid., p. 384.
17. Ibid., p. 259.
18. Ibid., p. 463.
19. *The Courage to Be*, Paul Tillich (Collins Fontana, 1962; first published Nisbet & Co, 1952), pp. 137ff.
20. *Etty: De nagelaten geschriften van Etty Hillesum 1941–1943* (Uitgeverij Balans, 1986), pp. 871–6.
21. *The Courage to Be*, op. cit., pp. 175, 176.
22. *The Boundaries of our Being*, Paul Tillich (Collins Fontana, 1973), pp. 280, 281.